# THE BLESSED VIRGIN MARY

# GUIDES TO THEOLOGY

*Sponsored by the Christian Theological Research Fellowship*

## EDITORS

Alan G. Padgett • *Luther Seminary*

David A. S. Fergusson • *University of Edinburgh*

Iain R. Torrance • *University of Aberdeen*

Danielle Nussberger • *Marquette University*

Systematic theology is undergoing a renaissance. Conferences, journal articles, and books give witness to the growing vitality of the discipline. The Christian Theological Research Fellowship is one sign of this development. To stimulate further study and inquiry into Christian doctrine, we are sponsoring, with the William B. Eerdmans Publishing Company, a series of readable and brief introductions to theology.

This series of Guides to Theology is written primarily with students in mind. We also hope that pastors, church leaders, and theologians will find them to be useful introductions to the field. Our aim is to provide a brief introduction to the chosen field, followed by an annotated bibliography of important works, which should serve as an entrée to the topic. The books in this series will be of two kinds. Some volumes, like *The Trinity*, will cover standard theological *loci*. Other volumes will be devoted to various modern approaches to Christian theology as a whole, such as feminist theology or liberation theology. The authors and editors alike pray that these works will help further the faithful study of Christian theology in our time.

Visit our Web page at

http://apu.edu/CTRF

# THE BLESSED VIRGIN MARY

*Tim Perry and Daniel Kendall, SJ*

WILLIAM B. EERDMANS PUBLISHING COMPANY

GRAND RAPIDS, MICHIGAN / CAMBRIDGE, U.K.

Published 2013 by
Wm. B. Eerdmans Publishing Co.
2140 Oak Industrial Drive N.E., Grand Rapids, Michigan 49505 /
P.O. Box 163, Cambridge CB3 9PU U.K.

Library of Congress Cataloging-in-Publication Data

Perry, Tim S., 1969-
The Blessed Virgin Mary / Tim Perry and Daniel Kendall.
p.        cm.
Includes bibliographical references (p.        ) and index.
ISBN 978-0-8028-2733-3 (pbk.: alk. paper)
1. Mary, Blessed Virgin, Saint — History of doctrines.
I. Kendall, Daniel.   II. Title.

BT610.P47   2013
232.91 — dc23

2012027780

www.eerdmans.com

# Contents

# Abbreviations

ACW     Ancient Christian Writers: The Works of the Fathers in Translation. Mahwah, NJ: Paulist, 1946-.

*ANF*   A. Roberts and J. Donaldson, eds. *Ante-Nicene Fathers.* 10 vols. Buffalo, NY: Christian Literature, 1885-1896. Reprint, Grand Rapids: Eerdmans, 1951-1956. Reprint, Peabody, MA: Hendrickson, 1994.

*CD*    Karl Barth. *Church Dogmatics,* ed. Geoffrey W. Bromiley and T. F. Torrance. Edinburgh: T. & T. Clark, 1956-1975.

FC      R. J. Deferrari, ed. Fathers of the Church: A New Translation. Washington, DC: Catholic University of America Press, 1947-.

LCC     J. Baillie et al., eds. The Library of Christian Classics. 26 vols. Philadelphia: Westminster, 1953-1966.

*LW*    Martin Luther, *Luther's Works* (American edition), ed. Jaroslav Pelikan and Helmut Lehman, 55 vols. Philadelphia: Fortress; St. Louis: Concordia, 1955-1986.

*NPNF*  P. Schaff et al., eds. *A Select Library of the Nicene and Post-Nicene Fathers of the Christian Church,* series 1 and 2 (14 vols. each). Buffalo, NY: Christian Literature, 1887-1894. Reprint, Edinburgh: T. & T. Clark; Grand Rapids: Eerdmans, 1952-1956. Reprint, Peabody, MA: Hendrickson, 1994.

PG      J.-P. Migne, ed. Patrologiae cursus completus: Series graeca. 162 vols. Paris, 1857-1886.

PL      J.-P. Migne, ed. Patrologiae cursus completus: Series latina. 217 vols. Paris, 1844-1864.

# Introducing Mary

## 1. A Brief Introduction to Mary

Why bother with Mary? At first glance, it's a simple question. She takes up relatively little space in the pages of Holy Scripture, is paid passing attention in the Creeds, embodies deep and persistent disagreements about doctrine and devotion across churches East and West, and Protestant and Catholic. Perhaps it is wiser to leave Mary alone for the sake of focusing on larger matters, where the possibility of ecumenical consensus is greater. Upon further reflection, however, the issues the question lays bare are quite complicated and therefore in need of further exploration.

The complications arise from the complex audience at which this book is aimed. Both audiences may have trouble with the question. And perhaps that's the best place to begin. On the one hand, we hope that people who read this book will be theology students — whether clergy or lay — from Protestant backgrounds, and especially evangelical Protestant backgrounds. For the first group, the question is to be directed at those Christians whose Marian doctrines and devotions seem to detract from devotion to Jesus. There is a sense in which this is a perfectly natural orientation to take up. After all, suspicion of all things Marian is part and parcel of the Protestant tradition from the second generation of the Reformation, and especially among those Christians whose roots extend to the Reformed half of the magisterial movement. It is certainly the way I (Tim) understood the question before I began to take a personal and scholarly interest in Mary in 2001.[1] As my work has progressed over the last seven years or so, the question has remained, but I have come to understand it differently. I find it being posed to me by groups of students, clergy, and laypeople who are fascinated by aspects of Christian piety quite foreign to them, and not quite clear what to do with it. I hope that the first group of readers will, as a result of this book, come to the same place — to recognize that the question needs not so much to be asked by us, but to be put to us. I hope to show to my Protestant fellow-travelers that we need to be — and indeed are becoming — more aware of the role Mary plays in theological conclusions that many of us take for granted.

On the other, we hope that it will also appeal to theology students — again, clergy or lay — within the Catholic and Orthodox churches. Unlike the first group, who may well wish to ask, but not be asked, for the second group, the question may in fact be unnecessary. Or perhaps it would be even better phrased negatively: Why *not* bother with Mary? She is such a part of the family furniture of the faith, so to speak, that it is impossible to think of Christian commitment without thinking of her, whether we are doing so in the contexts of doctrine (the Marian dogmas, ancient and modern), devotional practices (the Rosary, the Angelus, the invocation of the saints in prayer), or even art (iconography, the many portrayals of, e.g., the Annunciation in the history of Western painting). The temptation here may be, ironically, to take Mary and Marian issues for granted when precisely what is required is thoughtful engagement. This is especially the case because, since the Second Vatican Council, the Vatican has invited non-Catholic scholars to reflect with Catholic ones on the theological convergences and problems embedded in Marian doctrine and devotion, no less than three times.[2]

Why, then, should both of our major audiences bother with Mary? Our task as authors — one, an evangelical Anglican priest, the other a Roman Catholic, Jesuit priest — is to engage with this question from our own perspectives without necessarily presupposing where we will find common ground or what it will look like. We do so not to engage in debate or even in an exchange of views.[3] Rather, we hope to present — albeit in broad

---

1. See Tim Perry, *Mary for Evangelicals: Toward an Understanding of the Mother of Our Lord* (Downers Grove, IL: InterVarsity Academic, 2006), pp. 13-16 for a synopsis of that journey.

2. These invitations are contained in *Lumen Gentium*, chapter 8, Paul VI's *Cultus Marialis*, and John Paul II's *Redemptoris Mater*.

3. For such a conversation done in an honest and irenic manner, see Dwight Longe-

*Mary presentation / Jesus / Church / Indiv. Believers*

strokes — all the evidence from the Fathers to the present. In so doing, we hope that, as our readers engage with the same material and are directed to the same primary texts, they will also begin to talk to each other in a theologically informed way. Do we think we will single-handedly undo the Reformation? Hardly. But hopefully we will be able to show to all concerned that Mary does in fact matter if we are better to understand our shared theological heritage, our divergent theological developments, our radically different devotional practices, and our common commitment to Christ.

## 2. Marian Themes in Christian Faith

Because the historical narrative that follows attempts to cover almost two millennia of patterns of Christian thought and devotion, we thought it wise to introduce it in two related ways. After first highlighting the three broad themes that will reappear throughout the following essay, we will give a thumbnail sketch of Mary as she appears in the pages of the New Testament. We hope that this introduction will give readers some thematic and biblical framework on which to hang the chronological material coming later.

When examining Mary in the history of Christian thought, three intertwining threads ought soon to emerge for the discerning student: Mary's relationship to her Son (Christology), Mary's relationship to the corporate faithful (ecclesiology or the doctrine of the Church), and Mary's relationship to individual believers (Marian devotion or pious practices). Among these, of course, the first theme — Mary's relationship to her Son — is paramount. It is the driving concern, for example, of the first Christian thinkers, though not for the reason most readers might expect. The preoccupation of the ante-Nicene Fathers is not Mary's virginity — which is taken for granted as an indispensable part of the biblical story — but the reality of her motherhood. Mary really was Christ's mother; her humanity is his; he is therefore one of us. While the case can indeed be made that Christian thinkers have not always retained a good grasp on or understanding of the Lord's humanity, preserving that humanity as an integral part of Christology has remained an abiding concern in Christian thought until the present. And as a result, reflection on Mary has, too.

necker and David Gustafson, *Mary: A Catholic-Evangelical Debate* (Grand Rapids: Brazos, 2003).

3

Without detracting in any way from what has just been said, Mary has also functioned in the history of Christian thought as a sign of or pointer to the Lord's identity as the Second Person of the Blessed Trinity, and it is here that her virginity comes into view. Whether we are looking at patristic understandings of Isaiah 7:14 or Karl Barth's staunch defense of the *natus ex virgine* ("born of the Virgin Mary," taken from the Apostles' Creed), thought about Mary naturally arises when Christians reflect on the identity of the One she bore. Which brings us to the most important mariological term, *theotokos,* Mother or Bearer of God. Officially defined by the Council of Ephesus in 431, the term has a long history in both Christian and pre-Christian faith. Although it is a Marian term, within Christological discussions, it is intended to clarify the Lord's identity. From the instant of his conception, he was none other than the human instantiation of God the Son. He assumed all that being human is and means in a particular time, in a particular place, in a particular woman: Mary, the Mother of God.

Because of the One she bore, then, Mary is rightly understood to have a unique place both in the drama of salvation and in the lives of those caught in the wondrous story of God's love and grace. She is related to both Church and to individual believers. This recognition is as ancient as the faith, and finds displays in early Christian art as well as in early Christian thought and devotion. Some Fathers, as we shall see below, speak freely of Mary's relationship to the Church and locate that relationship in the asymmetrical relation between their respective virginal motherhoods. Both Mary and the Church are virgins insofar as they are pure and devoted to God; both are mothers as they bring forth God's children. The notion of Mary as a model of corporate faith is found in both medieval and modern theologians, but with different accents. For many medieval thinkers, the exaltation of Mary as model of the Church and especially of consecrated virginity was a strong temptation to decouple Mary from the rest of humanity. Instead of one of us to be emulated, she became the great exception to be adored. Against this view, many modern theologians, especially Catholic feminists, react most strongly. For it seems to them to enshrine over Christian women especially a hopelessly impossible ideal. A human woman cannot be both virgin and mother, and to expect imitation of and devotion to this ideal, they say, is psychologically and spiritually devastating.

The Reformers have their own reasons to be suspicious of these moves, for they seem to lead to disastrous theological consequences: (1) a loss of purchase on the mediation of Christ. If Christ is understood as our mediator with his Father, then the exalted Mary quickly becomes our mediator with her Son. Christ is thus removed from the experience of believers or worse, transformed into the angry Judge against which Luther in particular inveighed. (2) As Christ becomes removed or remote from our experience, further, Mary fills the vacuum — becoming, in the minds of some critics, not simply Christ's equal, working alongside him in the saving of souls, but even his rival who works to bend his will to her own. And yet, modern Protestants have been unwilling to jettison the tradition entirely, but, beginning with Karl Barth and continuing with Robert W. Jenson, seem open to trying to recapture the image of Mary as Type of Church, with sometimes surprising results.

It should be clear by now that it is very difficult in practice to distinguish between the last two themes. If Mary indeed is linked to the Church in a way unique because of her motherhood, she is thereby uniquely related to the members of that Church in an individual way. The notion of Mary as an intercessor — the greatest intercessor, indeed, among all the saints — again is ancient and certainly expands rapidly after the fifth century. In the medieval era, it seems that devotional practices led theological development — this appears certainly to be the case at least in early articulations of the doctrine of the Immaculate Conception. Likewise, in the first generation of the Reformation, it was specific devotional practices rather than Marian doctrines that aroused the Reformers' ire and even sarcasm. As we move to the modern era, diversity again comes to the fore. Marian devotions in the Catholic Church appear to wax and wane depending on matters of culture, geography, and time period. For Protestants, suspicion seems to be having to cohabit uncomfortably with a new mood of experimentation with forms of prayer — such as the Rosary — that would have been unequivocally condemned in the very recent past.

As we unfold the historical narrative of Mary in Christian doctrine and devotion in detail later, we hope that readers will keep these three themes constantly in view. They will enable readers better to understand the material by providing them with a different framework for organization. We hope, in other words, that thematic and chronological constructions will help readers to find, analyze, and assess different sets of interconnections between beliefs and practices as we tell the story of how the Church has thought about this extraordinary woman.

## 3. Mary in the Bible

When we turn to Mary as she is found in the pages of the New Testament, a distinct irony emerges. On the one hand, no other woman has influenced Western culture to the degree that she has. On the other, our only resources regarding her life amount to six chapters (two from Matthew and four from Luke), two stories in John, and scattered verses in Mark, Paul, and possibly Revelation. Undoubtedly, this paucity of material is what drives (some) Protestant concerns about so-called Mariology and its seeming over-emphases and departures from the biblical text. Still, when the texts are examined chronologically, a trend emerges, suggesting that the links between biblical texts and later developments are more than the tenuous results of pious eisegesis.

The first explicit reference to Jesus' mother is in Galatians 4:4, where Paul indicates belief in the Son's preincarnate existence and also unreservedly affirms Christ's humanity. "But when the fullness of time had come, God sent his Son, born of a woman, born under the law." In the mind of the early church, the preexistent Son entered the world in the most natural way — birth — and was here encountered as a human being. While we must be careful not to attribute too much to these assertions — e.g., awareness of the virginal conception or a full-blown Nicene Christology — we are introduced to a theme that will recur and expand over the next two millennia as Christians continue to think about Mary. Namely, she is the link between heaven and earth, the vehicle through which eternity entered time.

The earliest of the canonical Gospels complicates matters significantly in its apparent presentation of Mary as one of Jesus' opponents. In Mark 3:20-35, she and Jesus' "brothers" are presented along with the scribes who had come from Jerusalem as those seeking to silence him. She is not, however, culpable to the degree that the religious leaders are. They accuse Jesus of being in league with the Devil and are judged to have blasphemed the Holy Spirit as a result. Jesus' immediate family, on the other hand, seems to think that he is under some sort of demonic control, in need of restraint, and want to bring him home to Nazareth before harm comes to him. Mark's point — a theme running through his Gospel — is a poignant one. Good institutions, in this case, religion and family, can set themselves up against the Gospel. In Mary's case at least, they do so with the very best motives. Mary's opposition is to be read as positively against the entirely negative portrayal of the scribes. Furthermore, Mark straightforwardly presents her as the family-leader, with no mention of Joseph either here or elsewhere in the Gospel at all (cf. Mark 6:3).

It might seem that as we move from Mark into Matthew, and the first of two accounts of Jesus' conception and birth, that Mary might emerge more fully onto the stage. Such is not the case. In his account of Jesus' origins (chapters 1-2) Matthew appears to address questions surrounding the legitimacy of Jesus' messianic claim. Theologically, he addresses those who wonder how one whose parentage is questionable can claim to be the Messiah. Matthew counters that analogous sexually scandalous situations have already occurred in the messianic line. The genealogy insists that Jesus' messianic claim cannot be dismissed on a charge of illegitimacy while ignoring the scandal of Perez (Tamar), Boaz (Rahab), Obed (Ruth), and Solomon (Bathsheba). Mary's morals cannot be questioned without doing the same to Messiah's four foremothers. Second, both the genealogy and the birth story aver that even if Joseph is not Jesus' father, he is the adoptive father. Jesus' Davidic claim is intact. Finally, Matthew argues that Jesus' Davidic ancestry and messianic identity are devoid of scandal because throughout Joseph's dealings with Mary — both in the preempted decision to divorce her and the final decision to marry her — Joseph remains righteous. It is new information, not a change of intention, that causes the about-face. He is given an explanation for the facts in evidence: the child conceived in the womb of Mary is from the Holy Spirit.

Sociologically Joseph's righteousness also authenticates and alleviates any concern for those of the synagogue community scandalized by the social breach that is Mary's pregnancy. Matthew agrees that according to how things look, righteous people can, indeed should, be scandalized. Joseph is. Having assessed the situation according to all the information available, Joseph makes the decision to forego a public trial, and instead quietly divorces his betrothed. In this decision, Joseph is righteous. By presenting Joseph in this way, Matthew disarms those opponents confused by the claims of those following an "illegitimate" Messiah. He invites them to stand in Joseph's place, sharing the scandal that once confounded him. After thus legitimating their anxiety, Matthew asks what might have caused Joseph, the righteous man, to change his mind. Joseph's righteousness demanded he fulfill his social obligations. Only divine revelation concerning the true miraculous source of Mary's pregnancy could allow Joseph to look past the social breach and marry her. In this way, Matthew invites all righteous people to absolve Mary. He invites them to stand with Joseph, who, having received revelation, chose to make Mary's scandal his own.

Finally, Joseph provokes and resolves the political scandal aroused in Herod's court. The magi rightly recognize that Jesus is the "king of the Jews." Herod rightly realizes that this king challenges his rule. Even the Gentiles and the Idumean puppets of the Romans know who Jesus is. If Jesus is not righteous Joseph's adopted and therefore legitimate son, and David's heir, then he is no threat. Why then does Herod act like Pharaoh of old to destroy the child and his mother? Because Joseph is righteous, God can and does intervene in Joseph's life a second time in order that the child and his mother may find refuge in Egypt. The apologetic motif employed by Matthew is that of scandal. Theologically, he argues that such scandal is part and parcel of salvation history, running through the royal line from Judah to David; he argues through the birth narrative that beneath the appearance of social and political scandal is to be found the miraculous work of God. Accordingly, he adapts later Markan scenes to remove any notions of scandal arising within Jesus' family (cf. Matt. 12:46-50). Beyond a straightforward admission that Mary's pregnancy is by all appearances scandalous, we find out nothing about her. It is Joseph and more acutely, his righteousness that drive the plot.

Luke confers a new, higher status upon Jesus' mother, as reflected in Mary's three overlapping roles. The first is that of the prophet of the poor. Mary's prophetic office begins with her call (1:26-38), one that aligns her with Shiprah, Puah, Deborah, Jael, Esther, and Judith. She is presented as the climax of this list of female liberators, the one through whom the judgment and salvation of Israel will take place. She bears in her womb Israel's judge and savior. Her prophetic office is executed in the Magnificat (1:46-55) in which she declares that the God who has been mindful of her has always cared for the lowly and in such care, remembers and fulfills his promise to Abraham and the patriarchs. The second is that of the pondering mother. In Luke's account of the birth of Jesus and subsequent events, Mary does not fully understand all that is going on. Even though she is the unique recipient of divine revelation concerning Jesus' identity and destiny, the disclosure neither removes all ambiguity, nor resolves all struggle. Rather, it comes in bits and pieces — from the angel, Elizabeth, the shepherds, and even Jesus himself — and must be weighed and assembled over a long period of time. Her assent to the plan of God in the midst of all that is not understood is therefore to be commended.

8

*Introducing Mary*

It is only when Luke tells us that Mary was numbered among the first disciples awaiting Pentecost (Acts 1:14) that it becomes clear that Mary's willing assent persisted throughout her life. In the end, she did not change her mind. She continued to ponder the events she treasured in her heart for some three decades. She models, third, persistent discipleship that agrees to what is not yet understood because her confidence lies not in the revelation, but the character of the One who revealed.

Do these three distinct yet overlapping narrative functions testify to one overarching purpose for Mary within the Lucan narrative? There is such a literary purpose. Mary is Luke's symbol for God's people, whether defined as Israel or as the Church. Let us begin with the former. In the roles of prophet and mother, Mary is the specially elected crucible in which the general election of the nation of Israel receives its fullest expression. As a poor Jewish woman in first-century, Roman-occupied Palestine, Mary could have occupied no lower rung on the social ladder. Nevertheless, this same poor Jewish woman shared in God's election of Israel and in the purpose of that election: to be a blessing to "all the families of the earth" (Gen. 12:3). Divine election and its attendant gifts and responsibilities are hers as rights of birth. Mary alone, however, from all the women of the nation — whether at that time, before, or since — was specially chosen by God to be the vessel through whom the divine promises to the patriarchs would be fulfilled. Luke's account of the annunciation (1:26-38) gives no explanation for the rationale of God's election of Mary other than the fact that God is gracious. The favor bestowed upon her (1:28) is not a thing, but a description of the quality of her relationship with God that God had initiated. Indeed, Mary is not elected to a special vocation, but as the mother of the Messiah of Israel and the Savior of the world, to a *singular* vocation. Mary's election uniquely discloses the purpose of God's general election of Israel: through her prophetic speech, Luke's readers discover that it is through Mary's child that God's promises to Abraham and his descendants will be fulfilled (1:54-55). Accordingly the sword of judgment prophesied by Simeon (2:34-35) is both a sword of judgment passing through the land (Ezek. 14:17), causing the falling and rising of many in Israel, and a sword of judgment passing through the soul of Mary, disclosing her thoughts also. The winnowing visited upon Israel is the same as that visited upon the mother of Jesus. Just as the nation has been elected to bless the world, so has Mary. Just as the nation has been the recipient of divine disclosure, so has

9

Mary. Just as the nation will be judged by that same revelation, so will Mary. She is the daughter of Zion: a symbolic portrayal of the nation as a whole.

At the same time, she is a symbolic portrayal of the church. Here, however, she is not so much a "type" as an example of faith. Like all believers, Mary is the recipient of the good news of God's electing grace. Her confident assent to this sovereign choice is held up as an example, not of female acquiescence to the divine (male) Father, but as an example of the secure obedience that is to mark the lives of all disciples, whether male or female (cf. Gal. 3:28). Her daring adoption of the title "slave of the Lord" signals that she has freely accepted her role in the plan of salvation, a role that links her to the great liberators of God's people. She bids all disciples live in slavery to Christ wherein is found true liberation and vocation. Her confident obedience and free acceptance, moreover, is given not because of the clarity of the revelation, but because of her trust in the One who revealed. With respect to the content of God's disclosure, it appears her understanding is limited even as her will is determined to continue weighing matters until a coherent conclusion emerges. In the same way, all believers are to strive to trust in God even as they continue to ponder over the meaning of the divine revelation entrusted to them.

Mary is now a person. So sharply drawn is she, that it is possible to detect within Luke an emerging representative or symbolic role. It remains for the Johannine literature, however, fully to explore her symbolic significance. The Fourth Gospel and Revelation, regardless of whether or not they are related beyond anything other than the common name of their (traditional) authors, treat Mary as a highly developed literary device. The representative image first suggested by Luke has been significantly developed. In the Gospel, Mary symbolizes God's people, whether defined as church or synagogue. As the one who provokes the sign that foreshadows Jesus' "hour" (John 2:1-12) or who silently bears witness to it (John 19:25), readers are reminded of her command to the servants at the wedding: "Whatever he says to you, do it." She is a powerful reminder of the subordinate place of the people of God as those who point always and only to the One who, when his hour had come, redeemed the world. In Revelation, at least in its canonical context, Mary retains her corporate referent and indeed has it expanded. The seer even mingles images drawn from the Old Testament and those associated with pagan goddesses. As mother of the Messiah and the queen of heaven, she symbolically expresses the hopes and dreams not simply of Israel, but all humanity. These hopes are fulfilled in the victory of her Son over the Dragon.

There is tension here. On the one hand, Mary has been portrayed in the pages of the New Testament in such a way as to become a symbol for the corporate faithful. On the other, it is not at all clear that the exaltations rightly associated with the symbol — the heavenly queen, Eve (cf. 1 Tim. 2:15), the faithful of both the Old and New covenants, and so on — may be abstracted from their obviously figurative contexts in order to be applied in a more literalistic fashion to the handmaid of Nazareth. The legitimacy of such a move, which has surely taken place in the history of mariological developments, is not at all obvious at least at this point. The symbolic exaltation, however, cannot be denied. Indeed, the symbol of corporate faith is drawn so sharply that Mary the individual is overwhelmed.

This leads to a second observation: the Johannine portrayal of Mary *as an individual* is not that far removed from that of Paul with which this thumbnail sketch began. In both, they are anonymous. Whether she is Paul's mother of the heavenly man, John's mother of Jesus, or the seer's heavenly woman, we simply do not know much more about her as an individual. For both Paul and John, Mary's motherhood guarantees the humanity of he who entered existence from another, divine, kind of life. When Luke and the seer add deeper symbolic dimensions, using the mother of Jesus to disclose the theological significance of corporate faith, the purpose is to exalt Jesus, the Savior of all who are his. Mary is submerged in the symbolism that they have attached to her.

## 4. The Bible and Mary's Perpetual Virginity

We need, finally, to say something about how scholars differ in their understanding of some Scripture passages that treat Mary, and consider disputes that have arisen from diverse interpretations of those texts. Most Christians today accept the witness of Matthew's and Luke's Gospels that Mary was a virgin when Jesus was conceived. The main differences center around the question of whether or not she remained a virgin after Jesus was born. Mary's perpetual virginity is something that the Catholic and Orthodox churches strongly affirm (as did some of the early reformers such as Martin Luther), but some people today (including some Lutherans and Anglicans) have abandoned this position. The question arises because

Matthew's Gospel mentions that Joseph had no marital relations with her "until she had borne" Jesus (1:25), while Luke speaks of Jesus being Mary's "first-born son" (2:7). Furthermore, not only are "brothers and sisters" of Jesus mentioned in Mark 3:31-34 (with parallel texts occurring in Matthew 13:55-56 and Luke 8:19-21), but also Jesus' rather hostile "brothers" appear in John 7:3-5. Nowhere in the New Testament is Mary referred to as being "ever virgin" *(aeiparthenos)*.[4]

C. S. Mann remarks that a comparison "with a wholly different narrative (Luke 11:27f) seems to underline the possibility that on several occasions Jesus expressed ideas about true kinship as distinct from physical parentage or relationship."[5] He notes that with regard to the "brothers and sisters" question three early Church writers have taken three different positions:

"Brothers" are *blood* brothers. This goes back to Helvidius (c. 380) who first proposed it.

"Brothers" are sons of Joseph by a former marriage (Epiphanius, c. 382).

"Brothers" are cousins (Jerome, c. 383).

Jerome "based that on the assertion that *adelphos* could be used in Greek to indicate a far wider relationship than that of blood kinship. This was certainly true, but the Greek *anemsios* (cousin) was the regular word, and *adelphos* would hardly have been substituted for it."[6]

With such data in mind, let us briefly examine these texts. Matthew 1:25 does not deny Mary's perpetual virginity. In ancient Greek, the language of Matthew, "until" does not necessarily imply anything about what happened subsequently; it leaves the question open. Likewise the fact that Jesus was called her "first-born" (Luke 2:7) is somewhat ambiguous, since it could simply mean that Jesus possessed the rights and privileges of the firstborn son (e.g., Gen. 27; Exod. 13:2; Num. 3:12-13).

When Albright comments on Matthew 13:55-56 (and thus on the other parallel accounts), he says that we "know nothing of the brothers of Jesus. How old the tradition is we do not know, but it has been commonly held in both eastern and western Christendom, at least from the fourth century,

---

4. See Joseph Fitzmyer, *Luke I-IX* (Garden City, NY: Doubleday, 1981), p. 724.

5. C. S. Mann, *Mark* (Garden City, NY: Doubleday, 1986), p. 258.

6. Mann, *Mark,* p. 258.

that the brothers here referred to were either cousins, or children of Joseph by an earlier marriage."[7]

With the Gospels leaving the question of Mary's perpetual virginity unclear, we do better to reflect on the witness to the virginal conception of Jesus provided by Matthew and Luke. Gerald O'Collins explores its significance "not only for the revelation of God but also for human salvation."[8]

O'Collins distinguishes between the story of the conception and birth of John the Baptist from that of Jesus. In the latter case something new has happened in the history of the world. With Jesus God has come into the world in a special way. Jesus belongs to the Trinity, who has brought about a new creation.[9] His being, through the power of the Holy Spirit, conceived virginally points to the special role Mary played in the history of the salvation of the world.

## Conclusions

From this survey, two conclusions emerge. First, the New Testament's portrayal of Mary is diverse. For Paul, she is no more than an anonymous mother. For Mark, she is a misguided, well-intended opponent. For Matthew, the scandal surrounding her pregnancy must be explained if the messianic credentials of her son are to hold weight. For Luke, she is a prophet, a mother, a disciple, and perhaps even a representative of Jesus' new community. For John, she is a symbol of corporate faith which has no role in the ministry of Jesus, but becomes the mother of believers at the advent of his hour. In Revelation, she is the exalted heavenly queen who is Eve and the persecuted faithful all at once. The New Testament does not speak with one voice about this woman. It offers threads that further generations of Christians have, through their piety and theological reflection, woven into a tapestry that is at points theologically profound and at others, possibly, worrying. How best are we to think of the relationship among these diverse threads? The most helpful way to incorporate these threads is to see them in terms of development. The New Testament's witness regard-

7. W. F. Albright and C. S. Mann, *Matthew* (Garden City, NY: Doubleday, 1971), p. 161.

8. Gerald O'Collins, *Christology,* 2nd ed. (Oxford: Oxford University Press, 2009), p. 296.

9. O'Collins, *Christology,* p. 295.

ing the mother of the Lord developed over time from the truly minimal obscurity of the Pauline writings, through the ambiguity and scandal of Mark and Matthew, to the highly sophisticated, representational imagery of Luke, John, and the Revelator. It seems that as Christian proclamation spread throughout the ancient world, for whatever reasons, greater emphasis was placed in the theological significance of Mary's singular motherhood. Furthermore, the New Testament gives no indication that such development stopped with the closure of the canon.

Just as the first generations of believers pondered the significance of the mother of the Lord (as indeed they pondered the significance of her Son) so also will subsequent generations. This is inevitable as contemporary readers, along with those of the past, gather around the witness of Holy Scripture in order to discern not merely what Holy Scripture has said concerning her, but what it says.

## Select Bibliography of Monographs, Introductions, and Anthologies

Boss, Sarah Jane. *Empress and Handmaid: On Nature and Gender in the Cult of the Virgin Mary.* London: Cassell, 2000.

———. *Mary.* London: Continuum, 2004.

Boss, Sarah Jane, ed. *Mary: The Complete Resource.* New York: Oxford University Press, 2007.

Braaten, Carl E., and Robert W. Jenson, eds. *Mary: Mother of God.* Grand Rapids: Eerdmans, 2004.

Brown, Raymond. *The Birth of the Messiah: A Commentary on the Infancy Narratives in the Gospels of Matthew and Luke,* updated edition. New Haven: Yale University Press/Anchor Bible, 1999.

———. *The Death of the Messiah: From Gethsemane to the Grave: Commentary on the Passion Narrative in the Four Gospels,* new edition. New Haven: Yale University Press/Anchor Bible, 1999.

Coyle, Kathleen. *Mary in the Christian Tradition from a Contemporary Perspective.* Leominster, MA: Gracewing, 1996.

Gambero, Luigi. *Mary and the Fathers of the Church: The Blessed Virgin Mary in Patristic Thought,* trans. Thomas Buffer. San Francisco: Ignatius, 1999.

———. *Mary in the Middle Ages,* trans. Thomas Buffer. San Francisco: Ignatius, 2005.

Gaventa, Beverly Roberts. *Mary: Glimpses of the Mother of Jesus.* Philadelphia: Fortress, 1999.

Graef, Hilda. *Mary: A History of Doctrine and Devotion,* combined edition. London: Sheed & Ward, 1985 (two-volume original, 1963, 1965).

O'Carroll, Michael. *Theotokos: A Theological Encyclopedia of the Blessed Virgin Mary.* Dublin: Dominican Publications, 1982.

Pelikan, Jaroslav. *Mary Through the Centuries: Her Place in the History of Culture.* New Haven: Yale University Press, 1998.

Perry, Tim. *Mary for Evangelicals: Toward an Understanding of the Mother of Our Lord.* Downers Grove, IL: InterVarsity Academic, 2006.

Rubin, Miri. *Mother of God: A History of the Virgin Mary.* New Haven and London: Yale University Press, 2009.

Vassilaki, Maria, ed. *Images of the Mother of God.* Aldershot, UK: Ashgate, 2005.

Warner, Marina. *Alone of All Her Sex: The Myth and Cult of the Virgin Mary.* London: Vintage, 2000 (1976).

# I. THE HISTORICAL DEVELOPMENT OF MARIAN DOCTRINE AND DEVOTION

# 1. *The Fathers of the Church*

## The Pre-Nicene Fathers

In the outline of this book, it may appear to some readers that a disproportionate amount of space is devoted to the first five centuries of Christian thought on the subject. This approach, however, is deliberate. First, the Fathers are the heritage of the undivided Church. They teach all Christians, in both method and content, how to wrestle with the primary data of the Church's teaching, Holy Scripture. It is especially important for Christians who have come to disagree over substantial points of doctrine and devotion — and Mary is obviously one of these — to join at the feet of these early masters and learn together from them. The second reason is more complex. In Tim's research, he has found it common among modern theologians, both devotees and critics, to cite medieval theologians for a great deal of Marian teaching. It will become clear in later sections of this essay that this emphasis is legitimate; nevertheless, it lacks important nuance. For while medieval thinkers did clarify, deepen, and add intricate detail to previous mariological teaching, they did not innovate. The outline of Mariology — including matters on which Christians are divided — is found in the Fathers. Therefore, they merit greater attention.

We begin with **Saint Ignatius of Antioch (d. c. 110)**, an early Christian bishop and martyr. Like all Apostolic Fathers, Ignatius writes not as a theologian, but as a pastor concerned with the spiritual health of the congregations who may be subject to false teaching. He writes while a prisoner en route to Rome and to martyrdom. If we are to read his remarks about

Mary rightly, we need to keep the contexts of pastoral care and persecution firmly in view.

For Ignatius, Mary is first of all the guarantor of the union of divinity and humanity in Jesus' person. Thus, he affirms against those whom he believes to be false teachers that the "one physician" is "both from Mary and God" (*Ephesians* 7.2).[1] As the guarantor of his humanity, she is also, secondly, a sign of the reality of his suffering: "our God, Jesus Christ, was conceived by Mary according to the plan of God; he was from the seed of David, but also from the Holy Spirit. He was born and baptized, that he might cleanse the water by his suffering" (*Ephesians* 18.2).[2] The strongest statement is found in the letter to the Trallians, again in the context of rejecting false teaching (note the repetition of the word "truly," Greek *alethos*). "And so be deaf when someone speaks to you apart from Jesus Christ, who was from the race of David and from Mary, who was truly born, both ate and drank, was truly persecuted at the time of Pontius Pilate, was truly crucified and died. . . . He was also truly raised from the dead, his father having raised him" (*Trallians* 9.1-2). Finally, the letter to the Smyrneans makes a very similar declaration, but adds a new detail: Christ was "truly born from a virgin" (*Smyrneans* 1.1). Although Ignatius reveals little about the mind of the early Church, he yields information of tremendous importance. Mary is the key to the real humanity of Jesus. As really human, Jesus was baptized for us, suffered for us, died for us, and was raised to life for us. It is significant that while Ignatius affirms Mary's virginity at the time of Jesus' birth, it is not that miracle that assumes the foreground in his remarks. It is, rather, the miracle of the Incarnation: the one whom he describes as "our God" greets us, teaches us, and redeems us as one of us, as a human being. The close link between the motherhood of Mary, the humanity of Jesus, and the reality of salvation is one that will recur throughout the Fathers.

Early Christian leaders, it seems, hewed closely to the witness of the New Testament (such as they had it) in saying very little about the Lord's mother. The same is not true for the popular Christian imagination, where

1. Translations of the Apostolic Fathers have a standard citation system that resembles that of the New Testament. We follow that in our text. Translations are from the Ehrman translation in the Loeb Classical Library. Details can be found in the Annotated Bibliography.

2. See William R. Schoedel, *Ignatius of Antioch: A Commentary on the Letters of Ignatius of Antioch*, ed. Helmut Koester, Hermeneia (Philadelphia: Fortress, 1985), pp. 84-85, for a discussion of the linkage of the suffering of Jesus with baptism.

the paucity of biblical material provided fertile ground for legends to grow.[3] The ***Protevangelium of James* (c. 150)** provides a window into the early Christian imagination. The "protagonist" in this story is not Mary as much as it is her purity. The story's conflict revolves around challenges to its maintenance. Mary is conceived miraculously, in a manner similar to John the Baptist, her parents well aware that she has been called to a unique vocation (1-5).[4] Thereafter, her mother Anna preserves Mary's purity by raising her in a nearly sealed bedroom-sanctuary through which nothing "common or unclean" is permitted to pass (6). From the ages of two to twelve, Mary continues her rarefied life in the Temple (7-8) where, in a manner similar to Elijah in the wilderness, she receives "food from the hand of an angel" (8.1). At the onset of puberty, her Temple haven becomes a new threat to her purity. To maintain both the Temple and Mary from impurity, Mary is "married" to Joseph, an aged widower, and moved to his home (8-13). There, the Annunciation takes place (11). Now pregnant, the challenge to Mary's purity is obvious and overcome only through the judgments of a priest and Mary's cousin, Elizabeth (12), and a public trial of both Mary and Joseph (13-16). The final test is the child's delivery (17-20). The actual delivery is unobserved because it is veiled by God's glory (19.2). Nevertheless, through the story of the skeptical Salome, readers are informed that Mary has remained a virgin even here (19.2; 20.4).[5] This presentation of Mary as a near goddess figure did not fare well in the West, where it was harshly condemned by Jerome (see below). In the East, however, it proved to be especially popular. Its explanation of Jesus' siblings as Joseph's sons and daughters from his first marriage is accepted by the Orthodox family of churches to this day. Whatever the anonymous author hoped to achieve in his tale, he did not invent it. The popularity of his work suggests that he was drawing on streams of popular piety from the

---

3. Bruce Metzger, *The Canon of the New Testament: Its Origin, Development, and Significance* (Oxford: Clarendon, 1987), pp. 186-87.

4. Again, we refer to the standard "chapter and verse" citations. All quotations are from J. K. Elliott's translation. Publication details are found in the Annotated Bibliography.

5. Salome's declaration seems modeled after that of Thomas: "As the Lord my God lives, unless I insert my finger and test her condition I will not believe that a virgin has given birth" (19.3; cf. John 20:25). Where Thomas is content to believe Jesus' word and does not actually follow through on the Lord's invitation to touch his wounds, however, Salome does attempt to touch Mary and her hand is consumed by fire as a result, only to be restored by touching the infant Jesus (20.4).

early second century.[6] Its influence on later generations of theologians will become evident shortly.

**Irenaeus of Lyons (c. 140–c. 202)** draws upon a theme first enunciated by **Justin Martyr (c. 100–c. 165)** to highlight the unique place of Mary in Christian understandings of salvation.[7] Irenaeus's understanding of salvation draws heavily on Paul (cf. Romans 5; 1 Cor. 15) and is usually summarized in the word *recapitulation*.[8] Both Adam and Christ are understood to represent the human race. But where Adam disobeys and leads the race into sin and death, Jesus obeys, thereby rescuing the race and restoring life. Human beings may, because of Christ, recover their destiny and grow into the perfection for which they were originally intended. All creation will be regathered under one head (cf. Phil. 1:22; Col. 1:20). If Adam and Christ in this schema are to be juxtaposed, then in an analogous way, Mary is the new Eve who undoes the sin of the first. Both are understood to be married yet virgins, but where Eve's disobedience had led to slavery for the entire race, Mary's obedience — her agreement with Gabriel's announcement — brought freedom.[9] In fact, in a later passage, Irenaeus will go on to call Mary the "cause of salvation," over against Eve, who is the "cause of death." Mary is now Eve's "patroness."[10] Mary is no mere passive instrument in Irenaeus's thought. She actively, if subordinately, assists Christ in the accomplishment of salvation. She is "that pure womb which regenerates men unto God, and which he [Jesus] himself made pure."[11] This exalted language clearly exceeds the restraint of both Ignatius and the New Testament. Therefore, finally, two further observations need to be made. First, and more important, Irenaeus does not perceive or present himself as an innovator or devel-

---

6. Stephen Benko, *The Virgin Goddess: Studies in the Pagan and Christian Roots of Mariology,* Studies in the History of Religions 59 (Leiden: Brill, 1993), pp. 200-203.

7. Justin, *Dialogue with Trypho* 100 (*ANF* 1: 248-49).

8. The best summary of recapitulation in recent secondary literature is, in our view, Eric Osborn, *Irenaeus of Lyons* (Cambridge: Cambridge University Press, 2001), pp. 97-106.

9. Irenaeus, *Against Heresies* 3.22.4 (*ANF* 1: 455).

10. *Against Heresies* 5.19.1 (*ANF* 1: 547). In the surviving Latin manuscripts (the earlier Greek ones having been lost), the word translated patroness is *advocata*. An Armenian translation indicates that the Greek original may well have been *parakletos* (cf. John 14:26; Irenaeus, *Demonstration of the Apostolic Preaching* 33). The textual debate need not detain us, however. For our discussion, it is enough to note that in context, the word is intended to express recapitulation. Mary undoes what Eve did, or corrects her error.

11. *Against Heresies* 4.33.11 (*ANF* 1: 509).

*Taking stock in these writings b/c they were/lived so close to the time Jesus + Mary lived? Teaching what was first descended as the writing(s)?*

oper of the apostolic witness. He contends vigorously against the Gnostics that where they innovate, he stands in the tradition of the Apostles, having been trained by their first students.[12] Second, Mary is not so elevated as to be immune to fault.[13]

It is this latter point that is developed by Irenaeus's rough contemporary, the Latin Father **Tertullian (c. 155–c. 220)**. Indeed, the cranky North African apologist and theologian is an exception to the now established trend toward greater Marian exaltation. This is seen in four ways. First, where both Justin and Irenaeus contrast Mary's obedience with Eve's disobedience when enunciating the new Eve motif, Tertullian appears to downplay the women's activity, highlighting instead the contents and sources of their respective angelic messages: Mary believed God's truth; Eve, the Devil's lie.[14] Second, while Tertullian defends Mary's virginity as a matter of biblical record,[15] it is the reality of her motherhood — and consequently the reality of her Son's humanity — that receives more attention.[16] Third, Tertullian does not shy away from including Mary among Jesus' opponents prior to the resurrection[17] and from indicting her as an example of unbelief.[18] Fourth, Tertullian explicitly denies Mary's *in partu* and *post partum* virginity, both for the sake of the humanity of Jesus. Though Mary's womb was not penetrated by a father's semen when Jesus was conceived, it was in fact opened by a male, namely, her Son in the act of being born.[19] Jesus, truly human, was truly born. As for the latter, over against Gnostics who seemed to think that Jesus' rejection of his family (cf. Mark 3:31-35) was an assertion of his inhumanity, Tertullian avers that the text's reference to "brothers" means just that: Mary and Joseph had other children, each every bit as human as their eldest brother.[20]

---

12. *Against Heresies* 4.27.1 (ANF 1: 498; cf. Irenaeus, *Fragments from the Lost Writings of Irenaeus* II [ANF 1: 568]; Eusebius, *Church History* 5.20.5-7 [NPNF² 1: 238-39]).

13. *Against Heresies* 3.16.7 (ANF 1: 443).

14. Tertullian, *On the Flesh of Christ* 17 (ANF 3: 536).

15. *On the Flesh of Christ* 18, 20 (ANF 3: 537).

16. *On the Flesh of Christ* 17, 20, 21 (ANF 3: 536-39).

17. Tertullian, *Five Books Against Marcion* 4.19 (ANF 3: 378).

18. *On the Flesh of Christ* 7 (ANF 3: 530).

19. *On the Flesh of Christ* 23 (ANF 3: 541).

20. *On the Flesh of Christ* 7 (ANF 3: 530). See also *Five Books Against Marcion* 4.19 (ANF 3: 527-28; 3: 378) and *On the Veiling of Virgins* 6 (ANF 4: 31). He goes on to discern a moral quality to both roles. Mary as virgin and as wife distinctly hallows both celibacy and marriage as worthy Christian callings (cf. Tertullian, *On Monogamy* 8 [ANF 4: 65]).

On this point, a stronger contrast cannot be found than the Alexandrian theologian, **Clement of Alexandria (c. 150–c. 215)**, who affirms Mary's perpetual virginity as a biblical fact and as theologically significant. In *Stromata* 7.16, he alludes to the *Protevangelium of James* and quotes another apocryphal document, *Pseudo-Ezekiel*, as though they are Scripture — showing that the NT canon was not yet set at the beginning of the third century. In the same passage, Mary is presented as a model of the Scriptures which remain pure and yet give birth to truth, while in *Instructor* 1.6 Mary is a model of the Church, whose faith is intact and yet who brings forth many children. We thus detect an important shift in emphasis. Where the earliest Christian Fathers — while affirming Mary's virginity and the miracle of Christ's conception — tended to focus on the reality of Mary's motherhood as a sign of the humanity of Christ, in third-century Alexandria, Mary's virginity had come to be seen as having a theological significance in its own right.

This is confirmed when we consider **Origen (c. 185–c. 253)**, who while maintaining the Mary-Eve typology and stressing the reality of Christ's humanity, appears to have devoted more time to Mary's virginity. In part, this is apologetic — thus, against the pagan critic Celsus, Origen defends the virginal conception of Jesus and Mary's *ante partum* virginity.[21] But it is also a matter of biblical exegesis[22] and acceptance of received, nonbiblical tradition. One remark is worth quoting in full:

> Some say, basing it on a tradition in the Gospel according to Peter, as it is entitled, or "The Book of James," [i.e., the *Protevangelium*] that the brethren of Jesus were sons of Joseph by a former wife, whom he married before Mary. Now those who say so wish to preserve the honour of Mary in virginity to the end, so that the body of hers which was appointed to minister to the Word . . . might not know intercourse with a man after that the Holy Ghost came into her and the power from on high overshadowed her. And I think it in harmony with reason that Jesus was the first-fruit among men of the purity which consists in chastity and Mary among women. . . .[23]

---

21. Origen, *Against Celsus* 1.34 (*ANF* 4: 410-11).
22. Origen, *Homilies on Leviticus* 8.2 (FC 83: 155).
23. Origen, *Origen's Commentary on Matthew* 17 (*ANF* 9: 424).

These words are noteworthy for two reasons. First, the *post partum* virginity of Mary, as narrated in the *Protevangelium of James,* is defended not because the document is regarded as Scripture but because it is *fitting,* or in accordance with reason, that consecrated women have their own model of chastity. Second, where the intent of the author of the *Protevangelium* highlighted Mary's purity as a means of elevating Mary above humanity, Origen now appeals to it as an example of Christian asceticism worthy of emulation.[24] ↳ severe self discipline

It is fitting that Origen leaves us with a puzzle that is, given what textual evidence we now have, irresolvable. According to the early Church historian Socrates Scholasticus, Origen defended the term *Theotokos* (God-bearer or Mother of God) in a commentary on Romans a full two centuries before the Council of Ephesus defined the term and a full century before the earliest undisputed use of the word.[25] Sadly, the surviving versions of Origen's commentary do not contain the reference. Socrates' remark is an intriguing tidbit that certainly coheres with what we know about Origen's own Marian thought as well as that of Alexandrian Christianity's in general. It cannot be confirmed.

Whether Origen used the term or not, *Theotokos* was widely used by the time of **Athanasius (c. 295-373).** Its meaning was sufficiently clear that it could be used as a theological shorthand to defend a particular understanding of the Incarnation. Holy Scripture, says Athanasius, "contains a double account of the Saviour; that He was ever God, and is the Son, being the Father's Word and Radiance and Wisdom; and that afterwards for us He took flesh of a Virgin, Mary Bearer of God [*theotokou*], and was made man."[26] The one Savior is both God from all eternity and a human being, born of Mary. In Athanasius's theological writings, *Theotokos* language always arises in this Christological context and retains this Christological focus.[27] Further, in his *Letter to Epictetus,* a defense of the Nicene faith

24. Origen is well aware that this accentuation of Mary's virginity is complicated by the fact of her marriage to Joseph. On this point, Origen follows Ignatius of Antioch, contending that the marriage was the means by which God hid his plan of salvation from satanic opposition (cf. Origen, *Homilies on Luke* 6.4-5).

25. Socrates Scholasticus, *Ecclesiastical History* 7.32 (*NPNF*[2] 2: 171).

26. Athanasius, *Four Discourses Against the Arians* 3.29 (*NPNF*[2] 4: 409). For similar statements see, e.g., Athanasius, *Four Discourses Against the Arians* 3.31 (*NPNF*[2] 4: 410); *On the Incarnation of the Word* 8.2-3; 19.5; 37.3 (*NPNF*[2] 2: 40, 46, 56).

27. Indeed, Jaroslav Pelikan observes that the theological writings say nothing of sub-

*heresy that Jesus was not fully human*

against neo-Docetists, Mary functions as she did for Ignatius some three centuries before: her full humanity is a guarantee of Christ's humanity.[28] Rather than appealing to Scripture, however, Athanasius accuses his opponents of rendering "the commemoration and work of Mary . . . superfluous,"[29] thereby according church practice some sort of canonical status in determining correct theology.

Fortunately for English-speaking students, the core of Athanasius's Mariology lies in exhortations on the Christian ascetic life. *The Letter to the Virgins*, which is found in both Coptic and Syriac fragments, commends Mary as the ideal of consecrated virginity. The nuns to whom he wrote should "know [themselves] through her [i.e., Mary] as though through a mirror."[30] Mary's virginity *post partum* makes an ethical point: just as Mary had no other children after Jesus, so the nuns to whom he writes should follow in her footsteps, taking a vow of lifelong chastity.[31] Like her, they are to continue in various good works — generosity, devotion, modesty, and humility — thereby progressing in sanctification and showing themselves to be examples to others.[32] The detail with which Athanasius describes the life of Mary is, of course, impossible to verify against the sparse descriptions of Mary in Holy Scripture. Where does this portrait come from? Athanasius was not simply inventing a life. Rather, he was amplifying "the teachings of the New Testament on the basis of what had become explicit in the history of salvation since the New Testament."[33] The evidence provided by the lives of Egyptian monks and nuns — and recorded in his *Life of Antony*[34] — had, he believed, taught him the deep

---

stance about perpetual virginity beyond one passage that appears to deny virginity *in partu* (*On the Incarnation of the Word* 17.5 [*NPNF*[2] 4: 45]). Every occurrence of the word *aiparthenos* (ever virgin) in the Athanasian corpus is "either fragmentary or dubious or both." *Development of Christian Doctrine* (New Haven: Yale University Press, 1969), p. 99.

28. Athanasius, *Letters of Athanasius: LIX Ad Epictetum* 7 (*NPNF*[2] 4: 573).

29. A very similar remark is found the *Letter to Maximus*, where those holding that the Word became incarnate as a consequence of his Nature are told "if this were so, the commemoration of Mary would be superfluous." Athanasius, *Letters of Athanasius: LXI Ad Maximum Philosophum* 3 (*NPNF*[2] 4: 579).

30. S. Athanase, "Lettre aux Vierges," in *Lettres Festales et Pastorales en Copte*, trans. L.-Th. Lefort, Corpus Scriptorum Christianorum Orientalium 151 (Louvain: L. Durbecq, 1955), p. 59.

31. S. Athanase, "Lettre aux Vierges," p. 59, authors' translation.

32. S. Athanase, "Lettre aux Vierges," pp. 59-60.

33. Pelikan, *Development*, p. 102.

34. Athanasius, *Life of Antony* (*NPNF*[2] 4: 195-221).

meaning of the Bible's portrayal of the Mother of God. The ongoing life of the Church, in other words, continued to illumine the Scriptures by disclosing a meaning not explicit in the text alone.

By the watershed Council of Nicea, three key roles coalesced in the mind of early Christian thinkers. First, Mary was the guarantor of the reality of her Son's humanity. The Son of God, or God the Son, entered into human existence as a human being in the most average of ways: birth. Furthermore, Mary's humanity was itself understood to be unexceptional. While the miraculous nature of her Son's conception is accepted at face value, Mary herself could demonstrate impatience, lack of faith, and even doubt. At her best, she needed to progress in sanctification. Second, the acceptance of the title "new Eve" in the mind of the early Church suggests a role in the economy of salvation beyond her simple maternity. The early Church regarded her obedience to the call of God as that which undoes the disobedience of her foremother and ours. Finally, she was regarded as a type of the Church and an example for believers. Like the Church, she was the virgin bride who brought forth many children; her piety, chastity, hard work, and generosity were to be emulated by all who pursued the ascetic ideal. As we move into the post-Nicene era, these trends are deepened and begin to receive formal expression.

### The Post-Nicene Fathers

*act of becoming a greater a...*

When we turn to Christian Fathers writing from the later fourth through the eighth centuries, we find not so much an augmentation of the themes we have just encountered as their deepening. Thus, beginning in the East, the Cappadocians (**Basil the Great [330-379]**, **Gregory Nazianzus [329-389]**, and **Gregory of Nyssa [335-394]**) and **John Chrysostom (347-407)** all echo Alexandrian themes. First, Mary is presented as a sign of the reality of the Incarnation in its fullness — she is, in other words, a pointer to the true union of humanity and divinity in Jesus. Thus, with respect to the latter, Basil asks rhetorically, "if the God-bearing flesh was not ordained to be assumed of the lump of Adam, what need was there of the Holy Virgin?"[35] As for the former, Gregory Nazianzus adds the following: "He was born — but He had been begotten: He was born of a woman — but she

---

35. Basil of Caesarea, *Letter CCLXI: To the Sozopolitans* (*NPNF*[2] 8: 300).

was a Virgin. The first is human, the second Divine. In His Human nature He had no Father, but also in His Divine Nature, no Mother. Both these belong to Godhead."[36] So close is the connection between the sign (Mary) and the reality (the Incarnation of God the Son) that to deny the mother is to deny her Son:

> If anyone does not believe that Holy Mary is the Mother of God, he is severed from the Godhead. If anyone should assert that He passed through the Virgin as through a channel, and was not at once divinely and humanly formed in her (divinely, because without the intervention of a man; humanly, because in accordance with the laws of gestation), he is in like manner godless. . . . For both natures [divine and human] are one by the combination, the Deity being made Man, and the Manhood being deified or however one should express it.[37]

A right understanding of Mary thus ensures not simply a right understanding of doctrine, but also, in fact, salvation itself.

When we turn from the doctrine of the Incarnation to Mary's virginity considered in its own right, we find that for the Cappadocians, *ante partum* and *post partum* virginity are generally accepted as matters of biblical fact and hence, in need of little defense.[38] Virginity *in partu*, however, is a major concern. Basil, challenging those skeptical of the miracle, refers to the analogous conception of certain species of birds as a justification for "believing in the marvelous."[39] More subtly, Gregory of Nyssa argues that a painless delivery is itself a sign of the identity of the one so delivered. "It was indeed necessary that the mother of life conceive her child with joy

---

36. Gregory Nazianzen, *The Third Theological Oration. On the Son* (*NPNF*[2] 7: 308).

37. Gregory Nazianzen, *To Cledonius the Priest Against Apollinarius (Ep. CI)* (*NPNF*[2] 7: 439-40).

38. Students trained in original languages may wish to refer to Basil of Caesarea, *Homilia in Sanctam Christi Generationem* 5 (PG 31: 1468), where Basil comments on Mary's virginity as predicted in Isaiah 7:14 and fulfilled in Matthew 1:25. Similarly, John Chrysostom infers Mary's *post partum* virginity from Joseph's righteous character and Jesus' command to John from the cross; their marriage was necessary only to spare Mary the fate of an adulteress. See John Chrysostom, "Homily II," 1; "Homily IV," 5; and "Homily V," 5, in *Saint Chrysostom: Homilies on the Gospel of Saint Matthew* (*NPNF*[1] 10: 15, 22, 33).

39. Basil of Caesarea, *The Hexameron* 8.6 (*NPNF*[2] 8: 99).

and to perfect her act of giving birth in joy," he writes.[40] He also finds biblical support for virginity *in partu* in Exodus 3:1-6: from Moses' encounter with God, "we learn also the mystery of the Virgin: The light of divinity which through birth shone from her into human life did not consume the burning bush, even as the flower of her virginity was not consumed by giving birth."[41] Just as Christ, the light of the world, shone through the burning bush without consuming it, so he came into this world through the virgin without need of a regular delivery. John Chrysostom, on the other hand, affirms the miracle but shrouds it in mystery, describing Jesus' birth as "a new sort of travail, and a child-bearing so strange. . . ."[42]

Without a doubt, the apex of Eastern Marian development is found in the writings of **Cyril of Alexandria (378-444)**, whose understanding of Marian doctrine was enshrined and whose appreciation of Marian devotion was underwritten by the Council of Ephesus in 431. The Council itself was provoked by a conflict between the new patriarch of Constantinople, Nestorius, and the priests and parishioners of his diocese which erupted in December of 428 over the propriety of the by now well-established devotional Marian title, *theotokos*. Nestorius's objections to the title were, as far as we can tell, twofold. First, dogmatically, the title confused human and divine in the one man Jesus Christ by ascribing to the deity a measurable span of time. In short, the title erred by permitting such doctrinally silly sentences as "God is 33 years old." Second, liturgically the title had the unfortunate effect of underwriting forms of devotion that appeared to deify Mary and threatened to lead the Constantinopolitans into idolatry. He hoped to correct the course of both doctrine and devotion by proposing an alternative title, *Christotokos*, Christ-bearer, in order to clarify that Mary was the mother of Christ in his humanity only, and not in his deity. In hindsight, it is clear that Nestorius's attempt at reform could not succeed. Not only was *theotokos* too entrenched in piety to be overturned, but the term had been given a precise — and thoroughly orthodox — Christological formulation by the Cappadocians a century before. The most important factor was the theologically brilliant and politically hardnosed leader of the opposition: Cyril.

40. Gregory of Nyssa, *Commentary on the Song of Songs,* trans. Casimir McCambley, OCSO (Brookline, MA: Hellenic College Press, 1987), p. 237.

41. Gregory of Nyssa, *The Life of Moses,* trans. Abraham J. Malherbe and Everett Ferguson, The Classics of Western Spirituality: A Library of the Great Spiritual Masters, ed. Richard J. Payne (Mahwah, NJ: Paulist, 1978), p. 59.

42. John Chrysostom, "Homily V," 5 (*NPNF*[1] 10: 33).

For him, *theotokos* was, first of all, a dogmatic necessity. Cyril thought the Nestorian position advanced two sons, one Son of God and another son of Mary, the former impassible and immortal while the latter suffered and died. Remaining true to the Alexandrian linkage of salvation with assumption, Cyril countered that this denied the taking up of human nature by God the Son, leading invariably to the conclusion that God the Son was not born, did not grow, did not suffer, did not die, and did not rise again as a human being. In his mind, if God the Son did not fully enter into human experience in these ways, then he is not the Savior.[43] *Theotokos,* on the other hand, was a one-word summary of the Nicene faith, namely, that from the instant of his conception, God the Son assumed a human nature and in that human nature was born, grew, suffered, died, and rose again. Only *theotokos* could affirm the unity of the natures in one person. Accordingly, he writes: "we confess One Christ, One Son, One Lord. And it is with reference to this notion of a union without confusion that we proclaim the holy Virgin to be the mother of God, because God the Word was made flesh and became man, and by the act of conception united to Himself the temple that He received from her."[44] *Theotokos* directs believers to the mysterious union of human and divine in the one person in a unique and unsubstitutable way.[45] In the end, Cyril insists that Mary is not the mother of a nature — whether divine or human. She is mother of a person, and that person is the Son of God Incarnate.

Second, Cyril also maintained that the devotional forms associated with *Theotokos* were a fundamental part of authentic Christian worship. At the conclusion of the Council in which his views were vindicated, Cyril had this to say in his victory sermon:

> Hail from us, Mary, Mother of God, the venerable treasure of all the world, the inextinguishable flame, the crown of virginity, the sceptre of orthodoxy, the indissoluble temple, the place for the infinite, the Mother and Virgin; . . . Hail, the one who contains the uncontain-

43. Cyril of Alexandria, "Against Nestorius," in Norman Russell, *Cyril of Alexandria* (London: Routledge, 2000), pp. 131-32.

44. Cyril of Alexandria, *A Commentary upon the Gospel According to S. Luke by S. Cyril, Patriarch of Alexandria,* vol. 1, trans. R. Payne Smith (Oxford: Oxford University Press, 1849), p. 8.

45. Cyril of Alexandria, "Second Letter to Nestorius," in *Cyril of Alexandria: Select Letters,* ed. and trans. Lionel R. Wickham (Oxford: Oxford University Press, 1983), pp. 9-11.

able in the holy virginal womb, through whom the holy Trinity is glorified and venerated throughout the world, through whom heaven is exalted, through whom angels and archangels are delighted, through whom demons are banished, through whom the tempting Devil fell from heaven, through whom fallen human nature is assumed into heaven, through whom all creation, possessed by the madness of idolatry, came to the full knowledge of truth, through whom holy baptism came into being for all the faithful, through whom is the oil of exultation, through whom the churches have been founded for all the world, through whom the nations are brought to repentance. . . . Through whom the only begotten Son of God shined light for *those that sit in the darkness of the shadow of death;* through whom the prophets prophesied; through whom the apostles proclaim salvation to the nations; through whom the dead were revived; through whom kings reign, through the Holy Trinity. . . . The virginal womb; O thing of wonder! The marvel strikes me with awe! Who ever heard of a builder who, after he constructed his own temple, was prevented from dwelling in it? Who is insulted for having summoned his own servant into motherhood?[46]

Protestant readers especially ought to feel some sympathy with Nestorius at this point. For the points in Cyril's sermon at which we wince are precisely those where he did. All the more important, then, for us to see that the effusive Marian praise in this quote is never divorced from the mystery of the Incarnation. Nor is it ever equated with the worship due the Holy Trinity. Mary is for Cyril adored as the vessel through whom the Second Person of the Holy Trinity assumed our nature and in so doing, saved us.

As we leave the Eastern Fathers, readers both Catholic and Protestant might find it striking that alongside the very extravagant language used to describe Mary's place in the divine economy and the special significance of her perpetual virginity, the same authors appear to mention Mary's faults freely. Basil, for instance, affirms straightforwardly that, at the foot of the Cross Mary's faith lapsed.[47] Gregory Nazianzus, further,

---

46. Cyril of Alexandria, "Homily IV," translated in full as an appendix in Susan Wessel, "Nestorius, Mary and Controversy in Cyril of Alexandria's *Homily IV* (*De Maria deipara in Nestorium,* cpg 5248)," *Annuariam historiae concilliorum* 31 (1999): 42-49. See esp. pp. 43, 45.

47. Basil of Caesarea, *Letter CCLX: To Optimus the Bishop* 1.9 (*NPNF*[2] 8: 299).

speaks of Mary's need of divine purification in order to be a fit vessel for God the Son.[48] Far from being an exception to the rule that all have sinned and fallen short of God's glory, Mary's exceptional status is the result of a gift of purifying grace at or before the Incarnation.[49] Even Cyril could ascribe not only ignorance and doubt to her, but even suggests that she was scandalized by the humiliation of her Son at the cross.[50] The most explicit criticism comes from John Chrysostom. Not only does he speak freely of Mary's distance from Jesus as set out in the Gospels,[51] but he also suggests that her actions at Cana (John 2:1-12) display dispositions toward both vanity and pride.[52] Although the Western concept of original guilt is absent, there is a notion in these Eastern Fathers of original sin in which Adam left the entire human race condemned to death. Naturally, Mary shares in this condemnation. In and of herself, she is one of us and stands in need of the redemption provided by her Son as much as we do. It is only through the extraordinary working of the Holy Spirit that she is delivered from corruption such that the Son of God can assume her full humanity without thereby becoming contaminated by the disease of sin universally present after the fall of Adam. Lacking an Augustinian doctrine of original guilt, the Eastern Fathers do not need to exempt Mary from questionable conduct. For them, human beings are subject to physical and spiritual death because of Adam, but the guilt of Adam's sin is his own alone. In the Eastern view, an imperfect Mary is, because of her singular motherhood, worthy of all veneration appropriate to a created being.

It is precisely at these points that Western patristic Marian doctrine and devotion depart from the traditions of the East. On the one hand, it is immediately obvious in the work of **Ambrose (c. 337-397)**, **Jerome (331-**

---

48. Gregory Nazianzus, *Oration XXXVIII: On the Theophany, or Birthday of Christ* 13 (*NPNF*[2] 7: 349).

49. Gregory of Nyssa, *Letter XVII: To Eustathia, Ambrosia, and Basilissa* (*NPNF*[2] 5: 199-200).

50. Cyril of Alexandria, *A Commentary upon the Gospel According to S. Luke*, pp. 27-28.

51. John Chrysostom, *St. John Chrysostom: Commentary on the Psalms 1*, trans. Robert Charles Hill (Brookline, MA: Holy Cross Orthodox Press, 1998), p. 351.

52. On Mary's vanity, see John Chrysostom, "Homily XLIV," 1 (*NPNF*[1] 10: 278-79); though the reference is to John 2, Chrysostom is actually expounding upon Matthew 12:46-50. And on pride, consult John Chrysostom, "Homily on St. John XXI," 2, in *Saint Chrysostom: Homilies on the Gospel of St. John and the Epistle to the Hebrews* (*NPNF*[1] 14: 74).

Eastern view (point out Mary's faults) vs
Western view
*The Fathers of the Church*

419), **Augustine (354-430)**, and **Leo the Great (400-451)** that the Marian extravagances of the East are unparalleled. At the same time, however, they are just as reluctant to speculate about Mary's sinning. Even though Ambrose did affirm the doctrinal implications of the title *theotokos* in Cappadocian terms,[53] its Latin equivalent, *Mater Dei*, occurs only twice in extant writings while the more modest phrase, "the Lord's mother," is frequent.[54] Ambrose equally represents the Western reluctance to ascribe any sort of fault to Mary. For him, it is with a view to affirming Christ's full yet sinless humanity that Mary be both one of us and especially sanctified for her role in the drama of salvation.[55] Even at the foot of the Cross, Mary's faith remained unshaken. In words that seem consciously to challenge the East, Ambrose contends that:

> When the apostles fled, she stood at the Cross, and with pious eyes beheld her Son's wounds, for she did not look for the death of her Offspring, but the salvation of the world. Or perchance, because that "royal hall" [a title for the Virgin found elsewhere in Ambrose] knew that the redemption of the world would be through the death of her Son, she thought that by her death also she might add something to the public weal. But Jesus did not need a helper for the redemption of all, Who saved all without a helper. . . . He received indeed the affection of His mother, but sought not another's help.[56]

And yet, the departure from Eastern emphases is not entire. Indeed, when he turns to Mary as the monastic ideal, Ambrose is quite willing to borrow heavily from Eastern theologians for his own purposes. For example, his presentation of Mary as the ascetic ideal in *Concerning Virgins* is explicitly imitative of Athanasius's letter that we have already encountered. The following quote comes quite close to plagiarism: "Let, then, the life of

53. Ambrose of Milan, "On the Decease of Satyrus," 1.12 (*NPNF*[2] 10: 163). See also "Of the Christian Faith," 1.12.77-78 (*NPNF*[2] 10: 214) and "The Patriarchs," 11 (FC 65: 50-51); "Concerning Virgins," 1.5.21 (*NPNF*[2] 10: 366).

54. Ambrose of Milan, "Duties of the Clergy," 1.69 (*NPNF*[2] 10: 13) and "Concerning Virgins," 2.3.21 (*NPNF*[2] 10: 376).

55. Ambrose of Milan, "The Sacrament of the Incarnation of Our Lord," 9.104 (FC 44: 257). See also Ambrose of Milan, "On the Christian Faith," 4.9.114 (*NPNF*[2] 10: 277).

56. Ambrose of Milan, "Letter LXIII," 110 (*NPNF*[2] 10: 473).

Mary be as it were virginity itself, set forth in a likeness, from which, as from a mirror, the appearance of chastity and the form of virtue is reflected. From this you may take your pattern of life, showing, as an example, the clear rules of virtue: what you have to correct, to effect, and to hold fast."[57] Ambrose goes on, however, to speak of consecrated virginity in ways uniquely suited to his Western audience. It is, he says, a form of Christian life superior to marriage and widowhood.[58] This emphasis on consecrated virginity, of course, leads Ambrose to accentuate Mary's virginity in ways previously unparalleled in the West. Although he affirms Mary's *in partu* and *post partum* virginity, he treats them as miracles unique to the Mother of the Savior. When writing on asceticism, on the other hand, it is her *ante partum* virginity that is stressed, for it is here that Mary most resembles the nuns to whom Ambrose writes.[59]

At points, then, Ambrose exemplifies Western departures from Eastern patterns of thought and devotion, while at others he stands in continuity with them. He is at his most unique as a thinker when writing as an apologist for Mary's *in partu* and *post partum* virginity against Jovinian and Helvidius, respectively. Not all Christian thinkers, it appears, greeted the new monastic movement with enthusiasm. On the contrary, some feared that it was more Manichean than Christian in its apparent denial of, among other things, the goodness of creation, social responsibility, marriage, and sexuality.[60] Their champion was Jovinian, who suspected, among other things, that belief in Mary's *in partu* virginity concealed a denial of the Savior's full humanity based itself on a denial of the goodness of creation. He countered that since Christ was human, his birth was a fully human birth and accordingly and if so, then Mary really did lose her virginity in the act of giving birth. His point was not to reject asceti-

---

57. Ambrose of Milan, "Concerning Virgins," 2.2.6 (*NPNF*[2] 10: 374).

58. Ambrose clearly believes virginity to be a holier form of life than either marriage or widowhood. What is unclear is whether he means thereby to denigrate the latter two. "Concerning Widows," 4.23-24 (*NPNF*[2] 10: 395) contains remarks that seem to indicate that he does not wish to deny the goodness of marriage.

59. See, e.g., the description of Mary's life prior to the Annunciation as described in Ambrose of Milan, "Concerning Virgins," 2.2.9-10 (*NPNF*[2] 10: 74-75).

60. According to David Hunter, fourth-century "parents objected to losing their children to the monastic life; emperors opposed the flight of citizens who were escaping curial duties; even slaves objected to their masters' ascetic renunciation for fear of being sold on the open market." David G. Hunter, "Resistance to the Virginal Ideal in Late-Fourth-Century Rome: The Case of Jovinian," *Theological Studies* 48 (1987): 45-46.

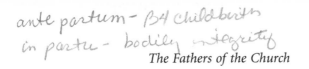

ante partum – B4 childbirth
in partu – bodily integrity

cism as a worthy Christian calling, but to oppose its presentation as a calling superior to that of married life. Ambrose's response was powerful: Mary's *in partu* virginity was a matter of biblical record, and does not deny the humanity of Christ but affirms the uniqueness of the Incarnation. Turning to the first matter, Ambrose's treatment of the New Testament is, unsurprisingly, sparse. He observes only that Isaiah 7:14 as cited by both Matthew (1:23) and Luke (1:31) predicts that the virgin will conceive — *ante partum* — and also will bear a son — *in partu*. The miracle is more clearly found in the foreshadowing of the Old Testament, both in Miriam's leading of the Israelites through the Red Sea[61] and in the prophet's vision of the closed outer gate of the sanctuary (Ezek. 44:2).[62] Further, far from denying his humanity, the miracle is a sign pointing to the unique nature of that *sinless* humanity.[63] It is at this point, however, that Ambrose seems to justify Jovinian's original complaint, for not only does he seem to hold that virginity is superior to marriage, but that sexuality in itself, even within marriage, is the occasion for the generation of original sin.[64]

If Helvidius wishes to make the same substantial points as Jovinian, he does so in a different way — by affirming that Mary had other children with Joseph after Jesus. His biblical argument is straightforward: this is the most natural way of reading those texts that refer to Jesus as Mary's *first-born* as well as those that speak of his siblings. Were this argument to win the day, however, Mary's role as the ascetic ideal would be undermined, for she did not, in the end, remain a virgin consecrated to God's service throughout her life. As a result, Ambrose responds again, this time reflecting on why a chaste marriage between Mary and Joseph is, in fact, the most natural reading of their life together. Ambrose offers six reasons: such a marriage would (1) preserve Mary's reputation; (2) legitimate Jesus in the eyes of the Jews; (3) permit Joseph to bear witness to her purity; (4) rescue Mary from having to hide her pregnancy through deception; (5) hide Jesus' identity from the Devil when he would have been most vulnerable to satanic attack; and (6) make sense of Jesus' charging John with Mary's care at

---

61. Ambrose of Milan, "Synodal Letters," 44 (FC 26: 228).

62. Ambrose of Milan, "On the Holy Spirit," 2.5.38 (*NPNF*[2] 10: 119). See also Ambrose of Milan, "The Patriarchs," 4.19 (FC 65: 252-53).

63. Charles William Neumann, *The Virgin Mary in the Works of Saint Ambrose*, Paradosis 17 (Fribourg: University Press, 1962), p. 161.

64. Ambrose of Milan, "Letters to Priests," 59 (FC 26: 332-33).

the Cross.[65] And having been entrusted to John, she did not "seek the consolation of being able to bear another son."[66]

Like Ambrose, Jerome follows in the Western tradition in two ways. First, Mary exemplifies Christian holiness.[67] Like Ambrose, Jerome insists that believers emulate Mary's surpassing purity: "Set before you the blessed Mary, whose surpassing purity made her meet to be the mother of the Lord."[68] The emergence of Pelagianism in the Western Church (the view that humans can earn salvation through their own obedience to God's Law), however, compels Jerome to insist more strongly that the purity for which God selects Mary is itself God's gracious gift.[69] Mary, even in her exalted state, needs grace, and precisely for that reason she can be held up for emulation. Second, Jerome's exaltation of consecrated virginity to a position superior to that of Christian marriage all-too-easily slips into the view that sexuality within marriage is evil. Consequently, Mary's virginity is sometimes presented as a necessary step in the creation of Christ's sinless humanity.[70] While both writers could insist on a connection between Christ's sinless humanity and Mary's virginity, however, the precise nature of that connection is unclear to them.

Jerome is also an important thinker in his own right. He is unique among ancient writers in insisting that his Marian beliefs are exclusively biblical. Thus the *Protevangelium of James,* so long an influential document especially in the East, is rejected because of its contradictions with the canonical accounts of the nativity.[71] St. Matthew's reading of Isaiah 7:14 is justified through a word-study of *'almah* as it is used elsewhere.[72] Following in the tradition of reading the Old Testament in the light of the New, Jerome found in the post-resurrection appearances of Jesus — entering through closed doors and leaving the tomb *before* the stone was rolled

---

65. See the full discussion in Neumann, *The Virgin Mary in the Works of Saint Ambrose,* pp. 184-235.

66. Ambrose of Milan, "Letter LXIII," 111 (*NPNF²* 10: 473).

67. See, e.g., Jerome, "Homily 93: On Easter Sunday" (FC 57: 247). See also Jerome, "Homily 88: On the Nativity of the Lord" (FC 57: 225).

68. Jerome, "Letter XXII: To Eustochium," 38 (*NPNF²* 6: 39).

69. Jerome, "Against the Pelagians," 1:16 (*NPNF²* 6: 457).

70. Jerome, "Letter XXII: To Eustochium," 19 (*NPNF²* 6: 29).

71. Jerome, "The Perpetual Virginity of Blessed Mary: Against Helvidius," 10 (*NPNF²* 6: 340).

72. Jerome, "Against Jovinianus," 1.32 (*NPNF²* 6: 370).

away — justifications for understanding the sealed fountain of Song of Songs 4:12 and the closed gate of Ezekiel 44:2-3 as allusions to Mary's perpetual virginity.[73]

He fully develops his understanding in the only book-length Marian work of the patristic era, *The Perpetual Virginity of the Blessed Virgin Mary: Against Helvidius.*[74] Unlike Ambrose, who largely speculated about the chaste marriage of Mary and Joseph, Jerome sought to meet Helvidius on his own, biblical, ground and show the latter's views to be simply silly. Where Helvidius proposed that Matthew 1:25 taught that Mary and Joseph enjoyed a full marriage, Jerome scornfully replied:

> I know not whether to grieve or laugh. Shall I convict him of ignorance, or accuse him of rashness? . . . If I choose to say . . . (as I certainly might) "Helvidius, before he repented, was cut off by death," . . . must Helvidius repent after death, although the Scripture says "In sheol who shall give thee thanks?" Must we not rather understand that the preposition *before,* although it frequently denotes order in time, yet sometimes refers only to order in thought? So that there is no necessity, if sufficient cause intervened to prevent it, for our thoughts to be realized. When, then, the Evangelist says *before they came together,* he indicates that time immediately preceding marriage, and shows that matters were so far advanced that she who had been betrothed was on the point of becoming a wife. . . . [It does not follow] that he had intercourse with Mary after her delivery when his desires had been quenched by the fact that she had already conceived.[75]

Should Helvidius then appeal to human experience, observing that to become betrothed but forego a proper marriage is truly exceptional, Jerome agrees and counters that he believes in the exceptional nature of Mary and Joseph's relationship because the Bible teaches just that.[76] In-

73. Jerome, "Letter XLVIII: To Pammachius," 21 (*NPNF*[2] 6: 78-79).

74. Jerome, "The Perpetual Virginity of Blessed Mary: Against Helvidius," 10 (*NPNF*[2] 6: 334-46).

75. Jerome, "The Perpetual Virginity of Blessed Mary: Against Helvidius," 4 (*NPNF*[2] 6: 335-36).

76. Jerome, "The Perpetual Virginity of Blessed Mary: Against Helvidius," 4 (*NPNF*[2] 6: 336). See also Jerome, "Homily 88: On the Nativity of the Lord" (FC 57: 224).

deed, since the Bible gives no reference to an alleged previous marriage, Jerome presents not only Mary, but also Joseph as a consecrated virgin. After all, only a righteous man — one uncontaminated by sex — would be a fit partner for the virgin.[77] It is likely his constant reliance upon the text of Holy Scripture that leads Jerome to treat Mary's *in partu* virginity gingerly. Of course, he does not deny it, for such would lead him to agree with Helvidius.[78] At the same time, however, he does not affirm it with the relish of St. Ambrose. At most, it is a mystery kin to the Risen Lord's entry into the house though the doors were locked (cf. John 20:19, 26).[79]

Without a doubt, the most important Marian thinker among the Western Fathers is Augustine of Hippo. As he draws upon the wealth of Christian teaching and adds his own distinctive contributions, Augustine gives Western Mariology its modern shape. Future debates — whether about the Immaculate Conception in the medieval era or the Bodily Assumption and the reforms of Vatican II in the modern — the form of Western Mariology has remained unchanged. This being so, it is important to note just how unexceptional the general shape of Augustine's Marian understanding is. Mary is "a virgin in conceiving, a virgin in giving birth, a virgin when with child, a virgin on being delivered, a virgin forever."[80] Further, he understands Mary to have taken a lifelong vow of virginity, a vow to be emulated by later generations of monastics,[81] and establishing the moral force of Mary's exemplary status. As a result, "Joseph might be called the husband of Mary, though she was his wife only in affection, and in the intercourse of the mind, which is more intimate than that of the body."[82] So plainly taught in Holy Scripture,[83] Mary's virginity needs no further argument to establish it. In fact, Augustine cautions against anything less than a full-blooded affirmation: "No one could say without vio-

---

77. Jerome, "The Perpetual Virginity of Blessed Mary: Against Helvidius," 21 (*NPNF*[2] 6: 344).

78. Though he does come very close when comparing Christ's birth with his death. See "The Perpetual Virginity of the Blessed Virgin Mary: Against Helvidius," 20 (*NPNF*[2] 6: 344).

79. See Jerome, "Homily 87: On the Gospel of John 1.1-14" (FC 57: 217-18).

80. Augustine of Hippo, "Sermon 186: On Christmas Day," 1, in *Sermons 184-229 (on the Liturgical Season)*, trans. Edmund Hill, OP, *The Works of Saint Augustine: A Translation for the 21st Century* (New Rochelle, NY: New City Press, 1993), p. 24.

81. Augustine of Hippo, "Of Holy Virginity," 4 (*NPNF*[1] 3: 418).

82. Augustine of Hippo, "Reply to Faustus the Manichean," 23.8 (*NPNF*[1] 4: 315). See also Augustine of Hippo, "Sermon I," 26 (*NPNF*[1] 6: 255) for similar remarks.

83. Augustine of Hippo, "Reply to Faustus the Manichean," 26.7 (*NPNF*[1] 4: 323).

lation of the Christian faith, that perhaps Christ was born of a virgin."[84]
All of this stands in the patristic mainstream.

It is when he turns his mind to understanding Mary's relationship at
once to her sinless Son and to the sinful rest of us that a curious inconsistency emerges that will help to define Western Marian debates for the next
millennium. On the one hand, he seems to contend against Manichean dualism of good and evil, spirit and matter, that Mary's virginity is neither
logically nor theologically necessary for the Incarnation to have taken
place: "The reason for our believing Him to have been born of the Virgin
Mary, is not that He could not otherwise have appeared among men in a
true body, but because it is so written in the Scripture, which we must believe in order to be Christians, or to be saved."[85] God did not need the Virgin but found it fitting to use her.[86] When contending against the Pelagian
notion that human beings can choose the good, however, Augustine concluded that the sin of concupiscence lay at the root of "original sin," the
disease passed from parent to child. Although concupiscence lies behind
every sin, it is so present in the sexual act that it is passed from parent to
child at the instant of conception. Accordingly, Christ must be conceived
in a way that prevents this concupiscence from being passed to his humanity.[87] "He came of this flesh, but He came not as other men. For the Virgin
conceived Him not by lust, but by faith."[88] Augustine leaves the inconsistency unresolved.[89]

He complicates matters further when he begins to wonder how, even
taking for granted the virginal conception, the Lord did not inherit his
mother's contaminated humanity. The question is straightforward. If
Mary is conceived such that her humanity is infected with original sin and
Mary really is Jesus' mother, such that her humanity is his, how does even a
virginal conception preserve Christ's humanity from the effects of the fall?
Augustine's answer is that Mary is saved in a way appropriate to her role as
the Savior's mother: "what He then took of flesh, He either cleansed in or-

84. Augustine of Hippo, "On the Trinity," 8.5.7 (*NPNF*[1] 3: 119).

85. Augustine of Hippo, "Reply to Faustus the Manichean" (*NPNF*[1] 4: 323).

86. Augustine of Hippo, "Sermon I," 3 (*NPNF*[1] 6: 246).

87. Augustine of Hippo, "On Marriage and Concupiscence," 13 (*NPNF*[1] 5: 269).

88. Augustine of Hippo, "Sermon XIX," 4 (*NPNF*[1] 6: 316).

89. Leo the Great, however, did resolve it, and decisively so. See Leo the Great, "Sermon
22: 25 December 441 (Recension B)," in *St. Leo the Great: Sermons*, 81-82 (FC 93: 81-82). See
also Leo the Great, "Sermon 24: 25 December 443" (FC 93: 93), for similar remarks.

der to take it, or cleansed by taking it. . . . He formed in order to choose her, and chose her in order to be formed from her."[90] As a result, Mary never actually sinned.[91] In short, Mary, like all human beings, stands in need of redemption but her redemption is uniquely accomplished in relation to her singular motherhood. In his reflections on Mary, sin, and salvation — imprecise though they may be — Augustine sets the stage for the famous medieval debates about the Immaculate Conception.

Finally, Augustine has a strong sense of the relationship between Mary and the Church. Both are virgin mothers,[92] to be sure, but there is more to it than that. As a believer, Mary is the sister of all disciples. At the same time, however, as Christ's mother, she is also maternally linked to all of his adopted brothers and sisters.

> And on this account, that one female, not only in the Spirit, but also in the flesh, is both a mother and a virgin. And a mother indeed in the Spirit, not of our Head, Which is the Saviour Himself, of Whom rather she was born after the Spirit: forasmuch as all, who have believed in Him, among whom is herself also, are rightly called "children of the Bridegroom": but clearly the mother of His members, which are we: in that she wrought together by charity, that faithful ones should be born in the Church, who are members of That Head: but in the flesh, the mother of the Head Himself.[93]

With Augustine, Western Mariology comes into its mature form. Mary is regarded as the perpetual virgin who, even as she stood uniquely in need of the salvation accomplished by her Son, was His sinless mother. Furthermore, she is intimately connected to the Church both as its prototype and as the mystical mother of all members of Christ's body. Whatever medieval (and, indeed, modern) developments take place, this fundamental shape will remain unaltered.

At the conclusion of this thumbnail sketch of the first five Christian

---

90. Augustine of Hippo, "A Treatise on the Merits and Forgiveness of Sins and on the Baptism of Infants," 38 (*NPNF*[1] 5: 60). See also Augustine of Hippo, "On the Gospel of St. John," 8.9 (*NPNF*[1] 9: 61), and Augustine of Hippo, "Sermon XIX," 4 (*NPNF*[1] 6: 316), for similar remarks.

91. Augustine of Hippo, "On Nature and Grace," 41 (*NPNF*[1] 5: 135).

92. Augustine of Hippo, "Of Holy Virginity," 2 (*NPNF*[1] 3: 417).

93. Augustine of Hippo, "Of Holy Virginity," 5-6 (*NPNF*[1] 3: 418-19).

centuries with Mary, what has been learned? We believe the following points are worth noting. First, Mary is not the central point of patristic theological debate. When she is mentioned — whether in Ignatius or Athanasius, the Cappadocians or Augustine — the central preoccupation is most often the clarification of Jesus' identity. Who is he? How is he related to the One he named Father? How is he related to us? These are the questions that fire patristic imaginations. Even as Augustine gave us the terms and problems that would become central in later debates about the Immaculate Conception of Mary, he does so not because he is worried about a right understanding of Mary's origins, but because he is driven to understand and to articulate as precisely as possible the identity of her Son. Second, this observation does not deny that as the patristic era progressed into the fourth century, Mary came to be associated with the emerging monastic movement, as its ideal or exemplar. On the contrary, it is in the context of emerging monasticism East and West that Mary is to some degree decoupled from Christological concerns and considered in her own right. It is in association with monasticism that Mary is first spoken of without direct reference to Jesus and, in fact, that the first book-length reflection (Jerome's *Against Helvidius*) on her significance is written. It is at this point, moreover, that we must acknowledge that especially Western Fathers, Ambrose and Jerome, at points displayed deep and irrational fears about human sexuality and especially female sexuality that did, unfortunately, eventually become part of the received tradition. Third, the drawing of parallels between Mary and the Church emerged early and persisted until the conclusion of the patristic era. If we compare Clement of Alexandria with Augustine, furthermore, it is clear that these reflections become more precise with the passing of time. Fourth, the Fathers approached Holy Scripture in a way very different from most of us. Very few modern readers would look at Solomon's sealed fountain or Ezekiel's closed gate and find therein references to Mary's perpetual virginity, and yet this was in no way a forced hermeneutic for the Fathers. Rather, because the Bible simply was the single presentation of God's saving communication, it was perfectly natural to read expecting not only that what was explicit in the New Testament should be implicit in the Old but also that the Old Testament especially should have multiple layers of meaning that yielded precious gems only to the most prayerful and careful readers. Finally, and most significantly, whatever the medievals did with Mary in the millennium following Augustine and preceding the Reformation, they did not invent. The scaffolding and much of the edifice that would come to be called Mariology was well in place before Bede, or later, Anselm and Aquinas. It is to that work that we now turn.

# 2. The Medieval Era and the Reformation

The second millennium saw the use of scholasticism as a way to organize philosophical and theological thought. Even among some groups today scholasticism is the usual method for expressing theological beliefs. Scholasticism attempts to reconcile apparently contradictory statements (whether from Scripture and/or reason) by using strict definitions of terms, dividing the material into categories, and then formulating arguments. Lawyers today follow this process. Obviously when this method is applied to theology, the results often appear similar to those of the legal document. Toward the end of the twentieth century one writer remarked that there is a difficulty "between the analytic language [of scholasticism] and the positive and nonexclusive language of the Scriptures and a formal or qualitative application of that truth."[1]

**St. Anselm of Canterbury (1033-1109)** was one of the first noted authors to employ this method to highlight "faith seeking understanding" (reason illuminating the content of belief). He used his famous "ontological argument" to prove the existence of God from reason alone. With regard to Mary, he reasoned that she was the mother of the re-created world. ("For God begot the Son, through whom all things were made, and Mary gave birth to him as the Savior of the world. Without God's Son, nothing could exist; without Mary's Son, nothing could be re-

---

1. Christophe Theobald, "The Church under the Word of God," in *History of Vatican II*, vol. 5, ed. Giuseppe Alberigo and Joseph Komonchak (Maryknoll, NY: Orbis; Leuven: Peeters, 2006), p. 312.

deemed.")[2] Seven hundred years later, in 1854, this argument would be expanded to the formal teaching of the Immaculate Conception by Pope Pius IX. What qualities were necessary for Mary to be the mother of Jesus? Strict reason would provide some type of answer.

Around 1099-1100, Anselm wrote a treatise titled *Of the Virgin Conception and Original Sin*. In this work like his others, Anselm wanted to show a rational basis for people's beliefs. Thus he avoided quoting Scripture and depended on reason to make his points. He began his argument by situating Jesus as a descendant of Adam and Eve. He mentioned that "it was expedient that he who was going to redeem the human race should exist and be born from the father and mother of all men."[3] He then reasoned as to why God chose to act in this way. "For it is absurd that Adam's sin, debt, and penalty should be passed down through a seed which is produced solely by the will of God — a seed which is not produced or brought forth by any created nature, or by the will of any creature, or by a power given by God to anyone else; for in order to beget a man by means of a new power God takes from the Virgin this seed which is free from sin."[4] He then added an argument ("it was fitting that this be so"), one that many scholastic theologians used. "Although the son of God was really conceived from the sinless Virgin, nevertheless it was not done by necessity — as if just offspring could not be begotten from a sinful virgin. But it was done because it was fitting that this man be conceived from a sinless mother." Anselm reasoned that when we consider who Jesus really was, then "it was fitting that the Virgin should be radiant with the greatest purity a creature could have."[5] He concluded that "even if sin pervaded the essence of the Virgin, nevertheless by means of faith the Virgin was able to become free from sin (in regard to the sinlessness of such a conception)."[6] What strikes one is that Anselm's point of reference is always Christ. Mary does not stand alone. When speaking of "original sin" he presumes the argument of Augustine that it is biologically passed on from parent to child. Once in a while, in speaking of Mary, he will use typology. For instance, in *Cur Deus*

---

2. Oratio 52; PL 158: 955-56.

3. Anselm of Canterbury, "Of the Virgin Conception and Original Sin," *Theological Treatises*, ed. Jasper Hopkins and Herbert Richardson (Cambridge, MA: Harvard Divinity Library, 1967), p. 22.

4. Anselm, "Of the Virgin Conception and Original Sin," p. 23.

5. Anselm, "Of the Virgin Conception and Original Sin," p. 28.

6. Anselm, "Of the Virgin Conception and Original Sin," p. 29.

*Homo,* he said: "Paint not, therefore, upon baseless emptiness, but upon solid truth, and tell how clearly fitting it is that, as man's sin and the cause of our condemnation sprung from a woman [Eve], so the cure of sin and the source of our salvation should also be found in a woman."[7] Again, he gave the argument of "it was fitting" to assert this.

Probably the most famous theologian of the Middles Ages was **St. Thomas Aquinas (1225-1274)**. Like others of his era, he wrote a *Summa of Theology* among his other works. To support his insights he used the philosophy of Aristotle. Most of Aristotle's writings had long been forgotten over the centuries. During the ninth and tenth centuries Islamic scholars in the Near East "rediscovered" texts of Aristotle in various libraries, especially the one at Alexandria. By the middle of the thirteenth century these texts were readily available in Europe. Aquinas's use of Aristotle's thought turned the emphasis away from Platonism and Neo-Platonic thought that had been so dominant in theological speculation. A glance at Aquinas's *Summa* shows how his mind operated. He gave arguments for and against a proposition, drew conclusions, and then answered opposing viewpoints. His mind worked like that of a lawyer. Like Anselm, he frequently used the "it was fitting" argument.

In speaking about Mary, Aquinas based her attributes on her relationship to her Son. Since her Son was divine, it was fitting that she should be adorned with the highest degree of purity in order that she might be conformable to such a Son.[8] This included a freedom from sin that none of the saints attained. She was cleansed from original sin though she was conceived in original sin.[9] This latter statement was forcefully challenged by Pope Pius IX in 1854 in his declaration of Mary's Immaculate Conception. Aquinas's view on Mary being conceived in original sin was short-lived and was abandoned by most scholastic theologians after John Duns Scotus (1266-1308). Aquinas, however, logically deduced that if Mary had been conceived without original sin, she would not have needed to be redeemed by Christ (and thus Christ would not be the universal redeemer).[10]

How was Mary cleansed from original sin? Aquinas referred to Jere-

---

7. St. Anselm, "Cur Deus Homo," in *Basic Writings,* ed. Charles Hartshorne (La Salle, IL: Open Court, 1962), p. 249.

8. St. Thomas Aquinas, *Compendium of Theology,* trans. Cyril Vollert (St. Louis: B. Herder, 1948), p. 263. This occurs in chapter 224.

9. Aquinas, *Compendium of Theology,* p. 263.

10. Aquinas, *Compendium of Theology,* p. 263.

miah 1:5 and Luke 1:15 to show that God had granted this favor to others. Would God have denied this favor to his own mother? Like the others, she was sanctified after the infusion of her soul, but unlike the others, her sanctification in the womb of her mother rendered her incapable of sin later on.[11] How did Aquinas arrive at the latter conclusion?

Aquinas believed that Mary never committed even a venial sin because she did not experience the inordinate motions of passion. Her sensible appetite was rendered subject to reason by the power of grace, which sanctified. The lower powers were so restricted by the power of grace that they were at no time aroused contrary to reason.[12]

Concupiscence played a large role in Aquinas's argumentation. He identified sin with concupiscence. This enabled him to assert that, as Mary grew in grace, concupiscence was weakened. After she had been made the shrine of the Holy Spirit and the tabernacle of the Son of God, there was never "any inclination to sin in her, [nor did] she ever [have] any pleasurable experience of carnal concupiscence." Thus she never had any type of sexual relationship with Joseph or bore any children other than Jesus.[13]

Obviously Aquinas had to deal with passages like Matthew 1:25 ("[Joseph] had no marital relations with her until she had borne a son, and he named him Jesus"), and Luke 2:7 ("[Mary] gave birth to her first-born son"). Aquinas's solution was to state that the "until" in Matthew's account does not mean a definite time but indeterminate time.[14] "First-born" in Luke's account does not necessarily imply other children. With regard to statements about Jesus' brothers and sisters (e.g., Matt. 13:55; Mark 3:32; Luke 8:20), Aquinas asserted that Mary's nephews and nieces are called Christ's brethren, as also are the relatives of Joseph who was reputed to be the father of Christ.[15] Here Aquinas appears to be relying on the *Protevangelium of James* to explain "Christ's brothers and sisters."

When Aquinas tackled the question of Mary remaining a virgin while giving birth to Jesus, he asserted: "Christ's body, which appeared to the disciples when the doors were closed [John 20:26], could by the same power come forth from the closed womb of his mother. It was not seemly that he,

---

11. Aquinas, *Compendium of Theology*, p. 204.
12. Aquinas, *Compendium of Theology*, pp. 265-66. Here begins chapter 225.
13. Aquinas, *Compendium of Theology*, p. 266.
14. Aquinas, *Compendium of Theology*, p. 266.
15. Aquinas, *Compendium of Theology*, p. 267.

who was born for the purpose of restoring what was corrupt to its pristine integrity, should destroy integrity in being born."[16]

We might draw some conclusions from Aquinas's treatment of Mary. He used Scripture as a person of the thirteenth century would. At times Scripture seemed to be a "prooftext" to solidify his argumentation. Augustine's influence appeared in connecting concupiscence with original sin, and was a presupposition of his logic. Aquinas gave an excellent example of the scholastic method. The arguments are so intertwined that one bad supposition is the father or mother of subsequent bad suppositions.

On the other hand, **Martin Luther (1483-1546)** preferred an Augustinian approach to theology rather than an Aristotelian one.[17] Though no single individual brought about the Reformation, a logical starting place would be to reflect on the background of the most famous person connected to it. According to the conventional story, Luther posted his ninety-five theses or statements to the door of the Castle Church in Wittenberg, Germany, on October 31, 1517. We can probably date the beginning of the Reformation to this real and symbolic act. Strikingly, Luther adds little to the discussion here, being happy to conform to the then-accepted Catholic teaching on Mary, affirming her perpetual virginity and holiness and affirming her identity as Mother of God throughout his life.[18] From 1521 onwards, there is a noticeable ratcheting up of the rhetoric against those forms of piety, especially Marian piety, that seemed to the Reformer to de-center Christ as the object of Christian devotion, or to present him as the wrathful Judge rather than the merciful Savior. In this, however, Luther was not unique. Thinkers within the Catholic Church, notably Desiderius Erasmus and St. Thomas More, expressed similar convictions, even as they lacked the German's unique volubility.

For subsequent generations of Reformation and post-Reformation theologians, however, Mary came to embody and express all that they perceived to be wrong with Rome. Where the Reformation saw salvation as a gift of God's grace alone, to be received by faith alone in Christ alone, Mar-

16. Aquinas, *Compendium of Theology*, pp. 267-68.

17. Much has been written on this issue. For instance, see Richard A. Muller, "Scholasticism, Reformation, Orthodoxy and the Persistence of Christian Aristotelianism," *Trinity Journal* 19, no. 1 (1998): 81-96.

18. The most important and extended of Luther's Marian reflections are found in his *Commentary on the Magnificat*. See Martin Luther, *The Sermon on the Mount and Magnificat, LW*, 21: 297-358.

ian belief and devotion presented salvation as a reward extended for a lifetime of grace-enabled and -aided effort, obtained from Christ through the mediation of the Church on earth and in heaven. From the second generation of the Reformation on, what few Marian remarks were made were colored with this polemical cast. At the same time, within the growing specificity and intricacy of Protestant scholasticism, reflection on Mary dwindled to finely tuned, small disputations about the necessity of the virginal conception of the Lord, whether the perpetual virginity of Mary could be biblically substantiated, and the propriety of the title *Theotokos.*

To meet the challenge of the Reformation, Pope Paul III convoked the **Council of Trent.** It first met in 1545, and held its last gathering in 1563. The Reformation inaugurated by Luther and the Council of Trent — two ironically similar reforming movements — symbolize two different emphases that would develop in the following centuries. Luther was a Scripture scholar, and he completed his translation of the Bible into German by 1534. It has influenced the German language like no other book. Luther's approach to theology from Scripture, especially his treatment of the writings of St. Paul, would dominate his many writings. When the Council of Trent met a few years later, it still used Latin as its official language. A glance at the formulations of its decrees shows the strong influence that scholastic philosophy and theology had on that Council, especially the authority of St. Thomas Aquinas. In the Council's fourth session (1546) a phrase appeared that cites Scripture and Tradition as sources of faith. "[Essential truths] are contained in the written books and unwritten traditions which have come down to us, having been received by the apostles from the mouth of Christ himself."[19] This innocent-sounding phrase marked the principal approach that would be taken by many Catholics toward their faith during the next four centuries: the dominant role of "tradition" (a concept not always well defined), while giving Scripture a subordinate role. The relationship between Scripture and Tradition was finally clarified at the Second Vatican Council (1962-1965).[20]

19. This translation is taken from *The Teaching of the Catholic Church,* ed. Josef Neuner and Jacques Dupuis, 7th ed. revised and enlarged (New York: Alba House, 2001), p. 102.

20. In his book *What Happened at Vatican II* (Cambridge, MA: Harvard University Press, 2008), John O'Malley says: "Vatican II . . . largely eschewed Scholastic language. It thus moved from the dialectic of winning an argument to the dialogue of finding common ground. It moved from abstract metaphysics to interpersonal 'how to be.' It moved from the grand conceptual schemes of summae with hundreds of logically interconnected parts to

Implied in Trent's teaching on God's revelation was a content larger in Tradition, at least potentially, than that of Scripture — "a content that could be 'developed' almost without limitation, as some theologians feared was happening with dogmas about Mary."[21] During the four centuries between the Reformation and Vatican II, Catholic theology developed with a greater stress on tradition than was to be found in Protestant theology. Yet that did not mean that Catholics had abandoned Scripture. Biblical roots remained very strong in Marian devotion: for instance, consider the Hail Mary (Luke 1:26-38), the Magnificat (Luke 1:46-55), and the Stabat Mater (a meditation of Mary at her Son's crucifixion), which were either recited or sung (in many settings) with musical accompaniment. Think too of the Rosary (reciting the Hail Mary while meditating on events and mysteries of Jesus' life and death), which was based very much in the New Testament story. Or again take Catholic art: so many paintings are of the Annunciation, the Nativity, and of Jesus being taken down from the cross. Catholic devotion to Mary has its New Testament roots.[22]

How did "tradition" operate with regard to Mary since the Reformation among Catholics? Scholastic methodology took as its starting point the Council of Ephesus (431). That Council declared that Mary was *Theotokos* (God-bearer, or Mother of God). Many theologians started with this definition and then applied reason and logic to arrive at qualities she "must" have. An analogy might serve as an example by looking at Christology. The starting point for theologians in the scholastic tradition is the Council of Chalcedon (451), which declared that Jesus was both divine and human. One only needed to apply logic to the meaning of "human" and "divine." Some conclusions people derived are that Jesus knew everything from the moment of his conception onward; he was omniscient. He never had any doubts or misgivings about his mission. Though this might be true logically and the argumentation might be quite coherent, theologians did not always ask themselves: "Do these conclusions agree with the evidence found in Scripture?" An overemphasis on a tradition that develops by itself and not connected with Scripture tends to bring about interesting

---

the humble acceptance of mystery. It modified the existing value system. It implicitly said, for instance, that it is more valuable to work together as neighbors than to fight over differences, as we have up to now been doing" (p. 46).

21. O'Malley, *What Happened at Vatican II*, p. 147.

22. For a good summary of these devotions see Gerald O'Collins and Mario Farrugia, *Catholicism* (Oxford: Oxford University Press, 2003), pp. 369-73.

conclusions. Such sometimes seems to have been the case with Marian devotions. Catholic theologians who came after the Reformation encountered Marian teachings that had been developed by people employing this deductive manner rather than using the inductive approach of the New Testament.

The Reformation began not long after the "discovery" of the New World. An event occurred in Mexico in 1531 that would profoundly influence the development of Christianity in the western hemisphere. At that time a peasant named **Juan Diego** had an encounter with Mary in what is now Mexico City. She appeared as a young, native pregnant girl who asked that a church be built in her honor at that site. The local bishop received Juan Diego with some skepticism when he presented his request. Juan Diego then went back to ask the Virgin for a sign so the bishop would realize that this was an authentic request. She told him to gather some roses growing at the top of the hill on that cold December day. Juan Diego did so, and put them in his tilma. The Virgin helped arrange them. When he returned to the bishop and opened his tilma to show him the roses, the Virgin's image was imprinted on the tilma. That tilma is on display in Mexico City to this very day. The Virgin of Guadalupe is part of Mexico's identity. Mexico's war of independence was waged under her banner, as were movements led by Miguel Hildalgo (1753-1811) and Emiliano Zapata (1879-1919). Even lottery tickets frequently bear her image. In 1945 Pope Pius XII declared her "Patroness of the Americas."

Since Mary appeared as a mestiza, devotion to her quickly gained popularity. She showed that God was interested in Mexico. Since early Mexico was formed from many different peoples and cultures — linguistic, ethnic, and cultural — she provided a common focal point for all of them. She is the mother of all Mexicans. This is clear today if one lives in or near a Mexican community. God has blessed Mexico and Mexicans by having his Mother, pregnant with his Son, appear among them. This was a very vivid way to teach the unsophisticated, mainly illiterate, audience of how great God's concern is for humanity (as expressed in Rom. 8:3; 1 John 4:9-11). It is always possible, however, for people to miss the point and venerate the Virgin to the neglect of God or the role of Jesus.

By the middle of the sixteenth century the scholastic approach was well in place and would influence Catholic theology for the next four hundred years. Very little new development occurred until Vatican II (1962-1965). It was in this atmosphere of scholasticism that people like **Francisco**

Suárez (1548-1617) and **John Henry Newman** (1801-1890) were to develop their approaches to Marian thought.

A glance at titles in the writings of Suárez shows him to have a very legalistic mind. He was a Spanish Jesuit who lived most of his life after the Council of Trent. The twenty-six volumes of his work covered topics such as metaphysics, relationships between Church and State, and areas of philosophy and theology. Of concern to us is his *Mysteria vitae Christi (Mysteries of the Life of Christ)*. This 1592 work "is important for its contribution to Mariology. About a third of the entire work is devoted to a study of the Mother of God and her prerogatives."[23] Suárez began with questions such as "Whether the Blessed Virgin Was Truly and Properly the Mother of Both God and Man" and "Why the Virgin Mary Cannot Be Called a Cause of God." One of the assertions that Suárez made was that Mary was chosen from all eternity to be the Mother of God "without reference to any foreknowledge of original sin. This is the unanimous teaching of those who maintain an analogous position on the predestination of Christ."[24] Thus he linked Mary's role to that of her Son. When Suárez treated the question, "Whether the Blessed Virgin by Conceiving Christ Lost Her Virginity or Corporal Integrity," he cited somewhat questionable historical material in formulating his reply. He asserted that "in her third year she had been offered in the temple and for eleven years had lived there among the virgins. For according to Cedrenus there was in the temple a secret spot, close to the altar, where only the virgins were accustomed to dwell. Among these virgins the Mother of God lived until her marriage. . . . Thus she remained a virgin from the time of her espousal to Joseph until the visit of the angel, as the words of the angel already quoted clearly prove."[25] Suárez cited Scripture to show that the virginity of Mary was clearly indicated. Texts to which he referred were Isaiah 7:14, Genesis 3:15, Psalm 131:11 [132:11 in most of today's Bibles], and Leviticus 12:2, as well as early Church Fathers.[26]

Mary remained a virgin during childbirth. To back up his position

23. Richard O'Brien in the preface to Francis Suárez, *The Dignity and Virginity of the Mother of God* (West Baden Springs, IN: West Baden College, 1954), p. vii. This book translated the first, fifth, and sixth disputations of the *Mysteries of the Life of Christ*, since "they treat what Suárez and most Catholic theologians consider Mary's fundamental privileges, that of Mother and Virgin" (p. ix).

24. Suárez, *The Dignity and Virginity*, pp. 23-24.

25. Suárez, *The Dignity and Virginity*, pp. 30-31.

26. Suárez, *The Dignity and Virginity*, pp. 35-40.

Suárez cited Isaiah 7:14 plus early Church writers (e.g., Irenaeus, Justin, Athanasius) as well as Aquinas.[27] He used a single text from Scripture (Ezek. 44:2) to back up his position that after childbirth Mary remained a virgin. In doing so he bolstered his arguments by referring to early Church writers such as Jerome, Augustine, and Tertullian.[28] He quoted Aquinas (among others) when he spoke of Mary retaining her virginity even though Jesus was her "firstborn," and that Joseph did not have relations with Mary "until" she bore her Son.[29] Likewise Suárez followed Aquinas's argumentation (and that of other early Church writers) that the "brothers and sisters" of the Lord refer to children of Joseph by a previous marriage, or they could be cousins or other relatives.[30] A glance at the sources referenced by Suárez shows us a theologian who had widely read both Scripture and the early Church writers. His writings show a strong scholastic approach to his interpretation of Scripture and faith.

27. Suárez, *The Dignity and Virginity*, pp. 45-58.
28. Suárez, *The Dignity and Virginity*, pp. 58-65.
29. Suárez, *The Dignity and Virginity*, pp. 62-65.
30. Suárez, *The Dignity and Virginity*, pp. 65-86.

# 3. Modern Contributions

## Modern Catholic Thought

In 1858, **Bernadette Soubirous**, a fourteen-year-old peasant girl living in a small town in southwestern France, claimed that a beautiful lady had appeared to her in a remote grotto. This "beautiful lady" appeared to her eighteen times and identified herself as the "Immaculate Conception." During one of those appearances the "lady" asked that people come in procession to the grotto. People who were sick and invalids began to visit the grotto. Some of them claimed to have been cured of their maladies by the water there. Franz Werfel wrote a novel that told of the occurrences at Lourdes. The movie based on this novel, *The Song of Bernadette,* won four Academy Awards in 1944. Today Lourdes is one of the world's most popular Marian shrines. In 2008 Pope Benedict XVI visited the shrine to commemorate the 150th anniversary of the appearances to Bernadette. Lourdes has a great appeal to people today.

Four years before Bernadette's experiences at Lourdes, **Pope Pius IX**, in 1854, had declared the dogma of the "Immaculate Conception." According to the language used by the Pope, "the doctrine which holds that the Most Blessed Virgin Mary from the first moment of her conception was, by a singular grace and privilege of Almighty God and in view of the merits of Christ Jesus the Saviour of the human race, preserved immune from all stain of original sin, is revealed by God and, therefore, firmly and constantly to be believed by all the faithful."[1]

1. *The Teaching of the Catholic Church,* ed. Josef Neuner and Jacques Dupuis, 7th ed. revised and enlarged (New York: Alba House, 2001), p. 284.

To back up this claim the Pope appealed to patristic tradition[2] and Scripture. Let us look at the document itself to see what texts from Scripture are cited to back up this claim. The Pope asserted that "the fathers and writers of the early Church" applied their interpretations of Scripture as providing a firm foundation for such a belief. For instance, Genesis 3:15 ("I will put enmity between you and the woman, and between your offspring and hers; he will strike your head, and you will strike his heel") is cited as a prophecy that shows Jesus is foretold as the Redeemer of humanity, and that Mary "united with him by a most intimate and indissoluble bond, was, with him and through him, eternally at enmity with the evil serpent, and most completely triumphed over him, and thus crushed his head with her immaculate foot."[3] Mary is compared to the Ark of Noah that was saved from shipwreck (Gen. 6:19), to Jacob's ladder that reached to heaven (Gen. 28:12), to the burning bush that Moses saw (Exod. 3:2), and so on. The main reason, however, for such a declaration was that "it was wholly fitting that so wonderful a mother should be ever resplendent with the glory of most sublime holiness and so completely free from all taint of original sin that she would triumph utterly over the ancient serpent. To her did the Father will to give his only-begotten Son — the Son whom, equal to the Father and begotten by him, the Father loves from his heart — and to give this Son in such a way that he would be the one and the same common Son of God the Father and of the Blessed Virgin Mary. It was she whom the Son himself chose to make his Mother and it was from her that the Holy Spirit willed and brought it about that he should be conceived and born from whom he himself proceeds."[4] In this proclamation, though a certain biblical basis exists, the Scripture references are secondary to the arguments from reason. Much like early Church writers, the Pope used the Bible more in a sense "accommodated" to his reasoning rather than what the original authors intended.[5] Catholics in the United States today celebrate the Immaculate Conception as the national feast of Mary.

---

2. Irenaeus, *Against Heresies* 3.3.2.

3. *Ineffabilis Deus,* the 1854 papal document announcing the dogma of the Immaculate Conception. This particular phrase occurs toward the end of the document where the paragraphs are not numbered.

4. *Ineffabilis Deus,* at the beginning of the document.

5. The "accommodated" sense is explained in Joseph Fitzmyer, *The Interpretation of Scripture* (New York/Mahwah, NJ: Paulist, 2008), p. 98. The Pope, however, was following early Church interpretations of Scripture.

**John Henry Newman** (1801-1890), declared blessed by Pope Benedict XVI in 2010, converted from Anglicanism to Catholicism in 1845. His career spanned the time before and after this papal proclamation. We can organize his writings on the subject of Mary into three separate categories: (1) the 1864 "Letter to E. B. Pusey" (The Belief of the Catholics, Mary the Second Eve, Sanctity of Mary, Dignity of Mary, Mary the Mother of God, Mary's Intercessory Power, Faith and Devotion),[6] (2) the 1849 *Discourses to Mixed Congregations* (Mater Dei, Mater Purissima, Refugium Peccatorum, Sine Labe Originali Concepta, Maria Assumpta, Growth of the Cultus of Mary),[7] and (3) the 1893 *Meditations and Devotions* (a posthumous collection of Newman's writings in which he commented on titles given to Mary in the Litany of Loreto).[8]

Let us look at these categories a bit more carefully. In his letter to E. B. Pusey, Newman made an important clarification when he titled an early chapter as "The Belief of Catholics concerning the Blessed Virgin, as distinct from their Devotion to her."[9] Though people might profess one and the same faith, he reasoned, devotion to her might be scant in one locale and overflowing in another.[10] In reviewing Church teaching on Mary, Newman began with the early Church Fathers. In them he found early belief in Mary as the second Eve. This imagery could be seen as early as Justin Martyr (120-165), and Newman traced this concept through the main authors of the Church's first 500 years. He then concluded: "I have drawn the doctrine of the Immaculate Conception, as an immediate inference, from the primitive doctrine that Mary is the second Eve."[11]

Newman referred to Mary as the woman clothed with the sun and moon as described in the book of Revelation (12:1-6). He explained his understanding: "Now I do not deny of course, that under the image of the

6. John Henry Newman, *Certain Difficulties Felt by Anglicans in Catholic Teaching*, vol. 2 (1892; London, New York: Longman, Green, 2001).

7. John Henry Newman, *Discourses to Mixed Congregations* (London, New York: Longman, Green, 1893).

8. John Henry Newman, *Meditations and Devotions* (Springfield, IL: Templegate, 1964).

9. Newman, *Certain Difficulties*, p. 26.

10. Newman, *Certain Difficulties*, p. 28.

11. Newman, *Certain Difficulties*, pp. 48-49. "Mary could not merit . . . the restoration of that grace; but it is restored to her by God's free bounty from the very first moment of her existence, and thereby, in fact, she never came under the original curse, which consisted in the loss of it."

Woman, the Church is signified; but what I would maintain is this, that the Holy Apostles would not have spoken of the church under this particular image, unless there had existed a blessed Virgin Mary, who was exalted on high, and the object of veneration to all the faithful."[12]

The Council of Ephesus (431) had declared that Mary was the "Mother of God." Newman commented: "This being the faith of the Fathers about the Blessed Virgin, we need not wonder that it should in no long time be transmuted into devotion. No wonder if their language should become unmeasured, when so great a term as 'Mother of God' had been formally set down as the safe limit of it."[13]

Newman also cited examples of intercessory prayer in the Scriptures to say that, once people have recognized the sanctity and dignity of Mary, they will realize that her office "is one of perpetual intercession for the faithful militant."[14] He acknowledged that excesses in Marian devotion have occurred over the centuries,[15] but he stated that faith has fallen off in places where "Jesus is obscured because Mary is kept in the background."[16] He noted that a glance at the prayers used in various devotions shows that Mary is looked at as an advocate for us, not as a source of mercy.[17] Intercessory prayer such as she gives for us has a long history in the life of the Church, and goes back to the Scriptures.[18]

Newman briefly looked at the teaching of Saints Basil, Cyril, and John Chrysostom about Mary's sinlessness. He admitted that two of the three thought that she actually sinned — the sin being that of doubt. This "sin" was to be attributed more to Mary's nature rather than her person. Yet, he asserted, individual views like these need to be viewed against the whole Church Tradition.[19]

*Discourses to Mixed Congregations* is a collection of talks given by Newman at various times to different audiences. Two of the chapters are titled "The Glories of Mary for the Sake of Her Son" and "On the Fitness of the Glories of Mary." He states that the point he will insist on, what is disputed by

12. Newman, *Certain Difficulties,* p. 58.
13. Newman, *Certain Difficulties,* pp. 65-66.
14. Newman, *Certain Difficulties,* p. 73.
15. Newman, *Certain Difficulties,* p. 89.
16. Newman, *Certain Difficulties,* p. 93.
17. Newman, *Certain Difficulties,* p. 101.
18. Newman, *Certain Difficulties,* pp. 69-73.
19. Newman, *Certain Difficulties,* pp. 135, 137.

people outside the Church but most clear to children of the Church, is that "the glories of Mary are for the sake of Jesus; and that we praise and bless her as the first of creatures, that we may daily confess him as our sole Creator."[20] Newman goes on to confess his belief in Jesus' humanity and divinity. Obviously, if God became a human being, then he must have had a mother. If Mary is the Mother of God, "Christ must be literally Emmanuel, God with us."[21] Son and mother go together. "As she was once on earth, and was personally the guardian of her divine child, as she carried Him in her womb, folded Him in her embrace, and suckled Him at her breast, so now, and to the latest hour of the Church, do her glories and the devotion paid her proclaim and define the right faith concerning Him as God and man."[22] That implies that she must be strong like the Tower of David, and witness to the world that God became a human being. Her prerogatives come from who her Son is. This includes her purity, her keeping the word of God. "Mary then is a specimen, and more than a specimen, in the purity of her soul and body, of what man was before his fall, and what he would have been, had he risen to his full perfection."[23] Newman continued: "It was fitting, for His honour and glory, that she, who was the instrument of His bodily presence, should first be a miracle of His grace; it was fitting that she should triumph, where Eve had failed, and should 'bruise the serpent's head' by the spotlessness of her sanctity."[24] Her intercessory power completes the enumeration of her glories. "If the Creator comes on earth in the form of a servant and a creature, why may not His Mother, on the other hand, rise to be the Queen of heaven, and be clothed with the sun, and have the moon under her feet?"[25] "Nothing is too high for her to whom God owes His human life."[26]

*Meditations and Devotions* were collected after Newman's death. The first seventy-eight pages are comments on the Litany of Loreto.[27] Newman

20. Newman, *Discourses to Mixed Congregations*, p. 344.
21. Newman, *Discourses to Mixed Congregations*, p. 348.
22. Newman, *Discourses to Mixed Congregations*, p. 349.
23. Newman, *Discourses to Mixed Congregations*, p. 352.
24. Newman, *Discourses to Mixed Congregations*, pp. 353-54.
25. Newman, *Discourses to Mixed Congregations*, p. 355.
26. Newman, *Discourses to Mixed Congregations*, p. 363.
27. This medieval series of titles and invocations of Mary was primarily used at the Italian Shrine of Loreto, but gradually was more widely used through the Western Church. They speak of her privileges, her holiness of life, her motherly spirit and queenly majesty. Examples of invocations include "Morning Star," "Refuge of Sinners," and "Help of Christians."

analyzed many of the titles in view of what qualities he considered Mary to have possessed. He added a lengthy memorandum "On the Immaculate Conception." Throughout the rest of the book he mentioned Mary in connection with other subjects about which he was writing. Since this book was devotional in character, his approach was to speak of attributes she must have possessed to be the Mother of Jesus, the Mother of God, an area that we have covered above.

Less than thirty years after Newman's death, in May 1917, just a few months before the end of World War I, Mary was reported to have appeared in Fátima, Portugal, to three Portuguese children, **Lúcia dos Santos**, and her cousins, siblings Francisco and Jacinta Marto, and urged them to make sacrifices and to pray for peace, especially by reciting the Rosary. These appearances took place over a period of six months. Mary also was said to have committed three secrets to the children: (1) a view of hell; (2) how to save souls from hell (consecration of Russia by the Pope to Mary's Immaculate Heart, and communion of reparation on the First Saturdays of the month); and (3) the assassination of the Pope and other religious figures. Francisco and Jacinta Marto died in the influenza epidemic of 1917. Their cousin, Lúcia, however, lived until 2005 when she died as a Carmelite nun in Coimbra, Portugal.

Sequels to the Fátima apparition included **Pope Pius XII** mentioning in a 1942 wartime radio address that he had consecrated the world to the Immaculate Heart of Mary.[28] A few years later (1948) he requested the consecration to the Immaculate Heart of Mary of every Catholic family, parish, and diocese.[29] These two events were minor, however, compared to what was to follow: the 1950 definition by Pius XII of Mary's Assumption, body and soul, into the glory of heaven. At the end of the document the Pope said that if anyone "dare to deny or call into doubt what We have defined, let him know that he has certainly abandoned divine and Catholic faith."[30] Let us examine how the Pope used Scripture to state so strongly that to be a Catholic one must believe this teaching.

The Pope began the encyclical by saying that God has arranged things so that all things may work together unto good for those who love him

28. *Acta Apostolicae Sedis*, 1942, 313.

29. *Auspicia Quaedam*, 22. This is the 1948 encyclical letter of Pope Pius XII.

30. Josef Neuner and Heinrich Roos, *The Teaching of the Catholic Church As Contained in Her Documents*, ed. Karl Rahner, trans. Geoffrey Stevens (Staten Island, NY: Alba House, 1967), p. 196.

(Rom. 8:28).[31] With the choice of Mary "when the fullness of time came," God put the plan of his providence into effect in such a way that all the privileges and prerogatives he had granted her in his sovereign generosity were to shine forth in her in a kind of perfect harmony (Gal. 4:4).[32] Since the time of Pope Pius IX (1792-1878) people had been asking popes to proclaim that Mary had been assumed into heaven.[33] After World War II had ended, Pius XII consulted the bishops of the world about issuing such a declaration.[34] They were the ones whom "the Holy Spirit ha[d] placed," he said, "to rule the Church of God" (Acts 20:28).[35] The bishops agreed that the Pope should make such a definition. This combination of the faith of the people and teaching authority of the bishops makes it clear that it should be taught infallibly. "Certainly this teaching authority of the Church, not by any merely human effort but under the protection of the Spirit of Truth (John 14:26) is clearly without error."[36] The Pope saw his role as that of "confirming the brethren in the faith" (Luke 22:32).[37]

The encyclical traced how belief in Mary's assumption had existed from the earliest ages of Christianity. Early Christians believed and professed "openly that her sacred body had never been subject to the corruption of the tomb, and that the august tabernacle of the Divine Word had never been reduced to dust and ashes."[38] Not only had churches been named after Mary's Assumption over the centuries, but early liturgical celebrations commemorated this.[39] Among the earlier Church writers who spoke about Mary's Assumption were St. John Damascene (676-749) and Germanus of Constantinople (640-733).[40] The Pope admitted that the Church had sometimes been very free about attributing biblical events and expressions to describe Mary. For instance, he said: "Thus, to mention only a few of the texts rather frequently cited in this fashion, some have employed the words of the psalmist: 'Arise, O Lord, into your resting place: you and the ark, which you have sanc-

---

31. *Munificentissimus Deus*, 1.
32. *Munificentissimus Deus*, 3.
33. *Munificentissimus Deus*, 10.
34. *Munificentissimus Deus*, 11.
35. *Munificentissimus Deus*, 12.
36. *Munificentissimus Deus*, 12.
37. *Munificentissimus Deus*, 19.
38. *Munificentissimus Deus*, 14.
39. *Munificentissimus Deus*, 15-17.
40. *Munificentissimus Deus*, 21-22.

tified' [Ps. 132:8]; and have looked upon the Ark of the Covenant, built of incorruptible wood and placed in the Lord's temple, as a type of the most pure body of the Virgin Mary, preserved and exempt from all the corruption of the tomb and raised up to such glory in heaven."[41] Other such examples the Pope cited were Psalm 44:10-14 [45:10-14] and the Song of Songs. The Pope added: "Moreover, the scholastic Doctors have recognized the Assumption of the Virgin Mother of God as something signified, not only in various figures of the Old Testament, but also in that woman clothed with the sun whom John the Apostle contemplated on the Island of Patmos [Rev. 12:1-6]. Similarly they have given special attention to these words of the New Testament: 'Hail, full of grace, the Lord is with you, blessed are you among women' [Luke 1:28], since they saw, in the mystery of the Assumption, the fulfillment of that most perfect grace granted to the Blessed Virgin and the special blessing that countered the curse of Eve."[42]

The Pope also quoted St. Anthony of Padua (1195-1231) as a source. "Among the holy writers who at that time employed statements and various images and analogies of Sacred Scripture to illustrate and to confirm the doctrine of the Assumption, which was piously believed, the Evangelical Doctor, St. Anthony of Padua, holds a special place. On the feast day of the Assumption, while explaining the prophet's words: 'I will glorify the place of my feet' [Isa. 61:13], he stated it as certain that the divine Redeemer had bedecked with supreme glory his most beloved Mother from whom he had received human flesh."[43]

After listing famous theologians who wrote since the time of St. Anthony (e.g., Albert the Great, Aquinas, Bernadine of Siena, Bellarmine, and Francis de Sales), the Pope concluded that "[o]nce the mystery which is commemorated in this feast had been placed in its proper light, there were not lacking teachers who, instead of dealing with the theological reasonings that show why it is fitting and right to believe the bodily Assumption of the Blessed Virgin Mary into heaven, chose to focus their mind and attention on the 'faith of the Church itself, which is the Mystical

41. *Munificentissimus Deus*, 26. The Scripture reference mentioned in the encyclical is to Psalm 131. Catholic Bibles often had a slightly different numbering system for the 150 Psalms. Today both Catholics and Protestants agree on the numbering that is found in the RSV and the NRSV editions of the Bible.

42. *Munificentissimus Deus*, 27.

43. *Munificentissimus Deus*, 29. Most Bibles today list the reference in the citation as Isaiah 60:13.

Body of Christ without stain or wrinkle' [Eph. 5:27] . . . and is called by the Apostle 'the pillar and ground of truth' (1 Timothy 3:15). Relying on this common faith, they considered the teaching opposed to the doctrine of our Lady's Assumption as temerarious, if not heretical."[44]

The Pope recalled Scripture and history to bolster his claim that Christians have held this teaching for over a millennium. "We must remember especially that, since the second century, the Virgin Mary has been designated by the holy Fathers as the new Eve, who, although subject to the new Adam, is most intimately associated with him in that struggle against the infernal foe which, as foretold in the protevangelium [Gen. 3:15], would finally result in that most complete victory over sin and death which are always mentioned together in the writings of the Apostle of the Gentiles [Romans 5–6; 1 Cor. 15:21-26, 54-57]. Consequently, just as the glorious resurrection of Christ was an essential part and the final sign of this victory, so that struggle which was common to the Blessed Virgin and her divine Son should be brought to a close by the glorification of her virginal body, for the same Apostle says: 'When this mortal thing hath put on immortality, then shall come to pass the saying that is written: Death is swallowed up in victory'" [1 Cor. 15:54].[45]

At the end of the encyclical the Pope summed up his arguments for defining this teaching. "Since the universal Church, within which dwells the Spirit of Truth who infallibly directs it toward an ever more perfect knowledge of the revealed truths, has expressed its own belief many times over the course of the centuries, and since the bishops of the entire world are almost unanimously petitioning that the truth of the bodily Assumption of the Blessed Virgin Mary into heaven should be defined as a dogma of divine and Catholic faith — this truth which is based on the Sacred Writings, which is thoroughly rooted in the minds of the faithful, which has been approved in ecclesiastical worship from the most remote times, which is completely in harmony with the other revealed truths, and which has been expounded and explained magnificently in the work, the science, and the wisdom of the theologians — we believe that the moment appointed in the plan of divine providence for the solemn proclamation of this outstanding privilege of the Virgin Mary has already arrived."[46]

44. *Munificentissimus Deus,* 35.
45. *Munificentissimus Deus,* 36.
46. *Munificentissimus Deus,* 41.

As we look at this encyclical from a scriptural viewpoint, we note that only eighteen footnotes (out of a total of forty-eight) reference the Bible. They frequently are not used in an exegetical way but rather in an "accommodated" sense. Although the Pope stated that this definition is based on both "Sacred Writings" and practice, most of the biblical quotations are not essential to the argument. The weight of the definition falls on tradition ("theological reasonings") that is "completely in harmony with other revealed truths." The conclusion is arrived at by a deductive process.

Subsequent to this encyclical, Pope Pius XII issued two more documents on Mary. One was *Fulgens Corona Gloriae* ("The radiant crown of glory") in 1953. The Pope reiterated the teachings on Mary's Immaculate Conception and her Assumption. He called them "very singular privileges" that were "bestowed on the Virgin Mother of God."[47] This use of the word "privilege" would open the way for a further development of the approach based on "tradition." A year later, the Pope instituted the feast of Mary, Queen of Heaven. In doing so, he said: "But the Blessed Virgin Mary should be called Queen, not only because of her Divine Motherhood, but also because God has willed her to have an exceptional role in the work of our eternal salvation."[48] He warned theologians that they should avoid two errors: "they must beware of unfounded opinions and exaggerated expressions which go beyond the truth, [and] on the other hand, they must watch out for excessive narrowness of mind in weighing that exceptional, sublime, indeed all but divine dignity of the Mother of God, which the Angelic Doctor teaches must be attributed to her 'because of the infinite goodness that is God.'"[49]

The death of Pope Pius XII on October 9, 1958, marked the end of one era in Catholic theology and the beginning of one that would be marked by a "return to sources." On January 25, 1959, the new Pope, **John XXIII**, announced that he was convoking an ecumenical council, the first in almost a century. **Vatican II (1962-1965)** was called to update Church teaching. At the beginning of the Council the Pope set forth its purpose and goals: "The greatest concern of the Ecumenical Council is this," he said, "that the sacred deposit of Christian doctrine should be guarded and taught more efficaciously. That doctrine embraces the whole of man, com-

47. *Fulgens Corona Gloriae*, 21.
48. *Ad Caeli Reginam*, 35.
49. *Ad Caeli Reginam*, 44.

posed as he is of body and soul. And, since he is a pilgrim on this earth, it commands him to tend always toward heaven. . . ." He continued: "Authentic doctrine . . . should be studied and expounded through the methods of research and through the literary forms of modern thought."[50]

Though many issues were discussed at the Council, we are interested in the role of Mary. Obviously among the almost 2,500 bishops who participated at Vatican II, opinions ranged from the very conservative to the quite liberal. A representative sample of the diverse viewpoints that were discussed included:

- Mary is mediatrix of all graces; Mary is co-redemptrix, a partner of Christ;
- The Council should provide definitions that would follow upon those of the Immaculate Conception and the Assumption, and clarify Mary's role, especially the "privileges" of Mary;
- Mary is the Mother of the Church;
- The purpose of the Council is not to define new dogmas about Mary;
- The Church had not always made serious inquiry about Marian apparitions, stigmatizations, and so on; Marian devotions had developed without reference to Scripture;
- Ecumenical considerations must play a part in any new statements; Protestant traditions must be considered;
- Mary must be included as part of the Church rather than be seen as above it.

The debate on Mary's role took place over a four-year period at the Council. The various proposals were ultimately grouped into two different approaches: (1) the Council should produce a unique document on Mary; (2) the Council should include Mary as part of another document, one on the Church. In either case, the Council needed to say something about Mary. These two approaches could be called the deductive versus the inductive (or scholastic contrasted with the historical-scriptural). Vatican II

50. This October 11, 1962, address *(Gaudet Mater Ecclesia)* inaugurated Vatican II. Subsequent history showed that scholasticism as a form of theological expression would diminish, and that biblical and patristic modes of thought would increase. This "return to sources" would affect Protestants as well as Catholics and refocused the consideration of Mary's role. See John O'Malley, *What Happened at Vatican II* (Cambridge, MA: Harvard University Press, 2008), p. 46.

would issue sixteen different documents on diverse areas. Let us examine the arguments for the two approaches to Mary.

On the eve of Vatican II the piety of Catholics was largely distinguished by their strong Marian devotion. Some even characterized it as "galloping mariology"[51] with little or no scriptural warrant.[52] Many bishops came to the Council hoping for a development of Marian doctrine. They saw "a further exaltation of Mary's role in the church as the reason for the convocation of the council and a new Marian doctrine as the culmination of its agenda."[53] Mary was not at the periphery, they believed, "but at the heart of Christianity: as the Mother of the Word Incarnate, Partner of Christ the Savior, Most Holy Mother of all the members of Christ, Universal Mediatrix, Virgin before giving birth, while giving birth, after giving birth."[54] In other words, using a deductive approach, "defenders of the 'privileges' of our Lady . . . analyzed the glorious titles of the Virgin as described in the encyclicals of the recent Popes"[55] and drew the logical conclusions from these premises. The proponents of this position believed that a document dedicated solely to Mary should be produced by the Council.

On the other hand, the inductive approach was characterized by a wish "to provide a more biblical and patristic foundation for Marian doctrine and piety."[56] Those who advocated this position believed that treatment of Mary should be part of a document on the Church. Several reasons were given: (1) Such an approach would avoid the objections against "an excessively institutional conception of the Church, which is in fact the community of the saved, on pilgrimage indeed but looking forward to an eschatological fulfillment prefigured by Mary."[57] (2) Historically, treating

51. Evangelista Vilanova, "The Intersession [1964-65]," in *History of Vatican II*, ed. Giuseppe Alberigo and Joseph Komonchak, 5 vols. (Maryknoll, NY: Orbis; Leuven: Peeters, 1995-2006), vol. 3, p. 369.

52. O'Malley, *What Happened at Vatican II*, p. 188.

53. O'Malley, *What Happened at Vatican II*, p. 188.

54. Joseph Komonchak, "The Struggles for the Council during the Preparation of Vatican II (1960-62)," in *History of Vatican II*, ed. Alberigo and Komonchak, vol. 1, p. 258.

55. Jan Grootaers, "The Drama Continues between the Acts: The 'Second Preparation' and Its Opponents," in *History of Vatican II*, ed. Alberigo and Komonchak, vol. 1, p. 480.

56. Joseph Komonchak, "Toward an Ecclesiology of Communion," in *History of Vatican II*, ed. Alberigo and Komonchak, vol. 4, p. 52.

57. Alberto Melloni, "The Beginning of the Second Period: The Great Debate on the Church," in *History of Vatican II*, ed. Alberigo and Komonchak, vol. 3, p. 96.

Mary as part of the document on the Church did "not mean reticence about Mary, but represented a position."[58] (3) Pastorally the faithful would be "encouraged to purify their devotion to Mary and to focus on what was essential to it."[59] Finally, (4) from an ecumenical point of view, "an ecclesio-typical Mariology made possible a convergence with both the Oriental and Protestant traditions."[60] At the end of four years of debate on the subject, the Council adopted this inductive approach. Mary was considered in light of the mystery of Christ and the mystery of the Church. It was by faith and obedience that she collaborated in human salvation as servant of the Lord (not as "associate" of the Lord). Mary is at the heart of the people of God as it makes its pilgrimage in faith and patience.

What were the practical results of this approach? (1) The Council centered piety on the Bible and the public liturgy of the church rather than on "devotions," including Marian practices, which often seemed to lead a life apart from Scripture and liturgy. (2) In the Council's teaching, scriptural language and concepts replaced those of scholasticism (and thus were more practical in everyday life). (3) There was a greater focus on Jesus. (4) Mary was considered as a loving helper and compassionate advocate for sinful human beings. (5) She is the "Mother of God" and Mother of us all, "who aided the beginnings of the Church," and "who intercedes with her son in the fellowship of the human family." (6) Thus her role is in the Church (the "fellowship of the human family").[61] The Council also warned theologians and preachers of the divine word to abstain zealously from all gross exaggerations with regard to speaking about Mary.[62]

The Council clarified the official position of the Church with regard to Mary in its document on "The Church." From what we have seen above, its approach was an inductive one that began with Scripture. This certainly appealed to Protestants who, since the time of Luther, had emphasized Scripture over a scholastic, deductive approach to theology.

In another document, the Council also clarified the Church's position on the relationship between "Scripture" and "Tradition," something left open by the Council of Trent. In explaining their close connection, the Council said that

58. Melloni, "The Beginning of the Second Period," pp. 96-97.
59. Melloni, "The Beginning of the Second Period," p. 97.
60. Melloni, "The Beginning of the Second Period," p. 97.
61. See chapter 8 of *Lumen Gentium* (Vatican II's 1964 document on the Church).
62. Chapter 8 of *Lumen Gentium*, 67.

both of them, flowing from the same divine wellspring, in a certain way merge into a unity and tend toward the same end. For Sacred Scripture is the word of God inasmuch as it is consigned to writing under the inspiration of the divine Spirit, while sacred tradition takes the word of God entrusted by Christ the Lord and the Holy Spirit to the Apostles, and hands it on to their successors in its full purity, so that led by the light of the Spirit of truth, they may in proclaiming it preserve this word of God faithfully, explain it, and make it more widely known. Consequently it is not from Sacred Scripture alone that the Church draws her certainty about everything which has been revealed. Therefore both sacred tradition and Sacred Scripture are to be accepted and venerated with the same sense of loyalty and reverence. Sacred tradition and Sacred Scripture form one sacred deposit of the word of God, committed to the Church.[63]

The same Pope who had presided over the last three (of the four) sessions of Vatican II, Paul VI, issued a document in 1974 on "The Right Ordering and Development of Devotion to the Blessed Virgin Mary." Its official title was *Marialis Cultus*. When introducing the document, the Pope stated that his purpose in issuing it "was precisely to restore and enhance the liturgy and to make more fruitful the participation of the faithful in the sacred mysteries." The Pope acknowledged that "certain practices of piety that not long ago seemed suitable for expressing the religious sentiment of individuals and of Christian communities seem today inadequate or unsuitable because they are linked with social and cultural patterns of the past." He divided the document into three parts.

In part 1 (paragraphs 1-23) the Pope reviewed the liturgical year with its various feasts. The Advent and Christmas seasons, he asserted, show a close link between Mary and Jesus. Commemorations such as the Annunciation (March 25) show Mary as the new Eve as well as being the Mother of God. Mary's Assumption (August 15) represents our anticipation as Christians to be ultimately with God. Mary provides a good example of our hopes as one who prayed with the Apostles and is a model of the Church. She is the attentive virgin who prays, has faith, and presents offerings to God (the Presentation of Jesus in the Temple). The Pope then asked people to revise their piety to Mary in light of Vatican II's declarations.

63. *Dei Verbum* (Document on Revelation), 2, 9-10.

After giving this framework, the Pope, in part 2 (paragraphs 24-39), set down some guidelines. Devotion to Mary should include Trinitarian, Christological, and ecclesial aspects. It should always be biblical, liturgical, ecumenical, and anthropological. He gave specific principles for each of these categories. Finally, in part 3 (paragraphs 40-57), the Pope spoke of two Catholic devotions, the Angelus and the Rosary. In this document the Pope implemented the decrees of Vatican II in a very practical manner.

Those people who can remember what Catholic devotional life was like before Vatican II can compare it to the present. Some contemporary examples include biblical prayer services replacing the recitation of the whole Rosary at funeral vigil services; homilies and sermons emphasizing Mary's link to Christ rather than speaking of Mary alone; a greater emphasis on community involvement rather than one that was strictly limited to individuals.

One of the leading theologians of the twentieth century was the Jesuit **Karl Rahner (1904-1984)**. He was an advisor at Vatican II and very influential in having Mary included in the document of the Church rather than treated in a separate statement.[64] Rahner has written so extensively that we sometimes have difficulty in following his thought on a single topic such as Mary. A small book written by him and another authored by his less famous Jesuit brother, Hugo, show us how they looked at Mary when the subject came up at Vatican II.

Hugo Rahner tips us off with regard to his approach to Mary in the introductory chapter of his book *Our Lady and the Church*,[65] published just before the beginning of Vatican II. That chapter is titled "Mary Essentially a Symbol of the Church." Rahner admitted the difficulties of the day: "It has not always been easy to fit together the somewhat subjective Marian piety, beginning with the Rosary and extending to the question of our Lady's universal mediation of graces and the devotion to her immaculate heart, with the essentially objective sacramental and liturgical piety involved in 'Devotion to the Church.'" The purpose in writing this book, then, was "to show from the warm-hearted theology of the great fathers and doctors that the whole mystery of the Church is inseparably bound up with the mystery of Mary."[66] The book is an elaboration of the funda-

---

64. See, for instance, the comments of Alberto Melloni, "The Beginning of the Second Period," pp. 96-98.

65. Hugo Rahner, *Our Lady and the Church* (New York: Pantheon Books, 1961).

66. H. Rahner, *Our Lady and the Church*, p. 3.

mental truth that undergirds the Church's teaching that "Mary, the mother of Jesus, in virtue of the ineffable dignity of being the Virgin Mother of God made Man, became the essential symbol of the Church, our Mother."[67]

Hugo Rahner sees the link between Mary and Eve as that of being the mother of the living. She gave birth to the living God. This idea is reflected not only in the book of Revelation, but also in writers such as Justin, Irenaeus, Hippolytus, Augustine, and Aquinas. "Eve, Mary, and the Church ... formed but one picture with three transparencies. Mary owes her position as the second Eve, and Mother of God's new human race, to her dignity as Mother of God; and similarly the Church owes her position to the fact of her being the mother of the Mystical Body of Christ, the mediatrix of divine life and the virgin mother of all ... whose life is in Christ." Thus Mary is the type or symbol of the Church.[68] "Everything that we find in the Gospel about Mary can be understood in a proper biblical sense of the mystery of the Church."[69] After Rahner had established his position, he then applied it to various titles attributed to Mary.

Mary is called "immaculate" because "from the sources of Revelation and from the solemn declaration of the Church, namely that ... in the first instant of her conception, in virtue of the redemptive death to come of her divine son, [she] was preserved free from all stain of original sin." Thus she possessed from the beginning of her life that gift of sanctifying grace "which was destined originally for the whole human race from Adam and Eve, and restored to every believer by the death of Christ, the son of Mary. Thus it is that Mary Immaculate is already an essential symbol of the restoration to grace."[70] She is a figure of the Church, "for the Church is the fulfillment of the history that began at Mary's conception, anticipating the redeeming sacrifice, and ends with the admission of Adam's race to eternal life, with the Father, through the Son and in the Holy Ghost."[71]

Mary is "ever virgin," since the "idea of her divine motherhood is completed by the further grace of her virginal conception of our Lord and her subsequent ever virginal state."[72] After Rahner had reviewed what vari-

67. H. Rahner, *Our Lady and the Church*, p. 4.
68. H. Rahner, *Our Lady and the Church*, p. 5.
69. H. Rahner, *Our Lady and the Church*, p. 10.
70. H. Rahner, *Our Lady and the Church*, p. 13.
71. H. Rahner, *Our Lady and the Church*, p. 15.
72. H. Rahner, *Our Lady and the Church*, p. 22.

ous writers over the centuries have said about Mary's perpetual virginity, he applied it to the Church. Heretics are those who have lost their virginity; error can enter the local Church and rob that Church of her virginity. But when the early Church says that Mary is ever a virgin and can never fall into Eve's unfaithfulness, it "is in fact saying neither more nor less than we say today with our doctrine of the Church's infallibility."[73]

Mary, the symbol of the Church, is also the Mother of God. "In the teaching of the fathers we find that not only is the virgin Church truly a mother because she has given birth to us, the many, into everlasting life, but also because she is 'the Mother of God' in that she is ever giving new life to the Mystical Body of Christ. In the mystery she is the mother of the one and the whole Christ."[74]

Hugo Rahner also spoke of the other titles of Mary. She is "Mother of the Faithful." Because of her position as the Mother of God, "she stands indeed in a special relationship to all mankind who have been formed into a single body through the power of the redeeming blood of her son: Mary is truly the mother of all the redeemed."[75] She is the "Woman of the Apocalypse." In her new life above, "she has a powerful influence on earthly affairs, and is at last revealed as what she truly is. Mary, in a way corresponding to the glorious risen life of our Lord, has been transformed into a being that is of both heaven and earth; no longer now the 'handmaid,' for 'behold from henceforth all generations shall call me blessed.'"[76]

In his book *Mary the Mother of the Lord*,[77] published during Vatican II, Karl Rahner repeated most of the same material. He set out his basic outline by saying that "Mary is the virgin Mother of Jesus Christ. The meaning of this statement, and the fact that it says everything about her, becomes clear, if one considers whose mother she is, and in what way she is his mother."[78] One chapter that stands out, however, is that in which he treated the controversial issue: "Mediatrix of Graces." Rahner says that this phrase is "in customary use in the Church, though it does not embody a defined truth in the strict sense. We can simply say that Mary is our mediatrix. After all we have often prayed to our Lady as our advocate, our

---

73. H. Rahner, *Our Lady and the Church*, p. 25.
74. H. Rahner, *Our Lady and the Church*, p. 33.
75. H. Rahner, *Our Lady and the Church*, p. 43.
76. H. Rahner, *Our Lady and the Church*, p. 103.
77. Karl Rahner, *Mary the Mother of the Lord* (New York: Herder & Herder, 1963).
78. K. Rahner, *Mary the Mother of the Lord*, p. 9.

intercessor."[79] He realized that people would say that Jesus Christ is our mediator, the only mediator between God and ourselves. To that objection he replied: "And to this question, propounded in this form, are we not obliged to answer, as a matter of course, with a plain, unqualified YES?"[80] "He it is, therefore, who by what he is and what he does, forms the one unique unifying bond between God and his creation that is to be redeemed. In this sense he is the unique mediator."[81] Rahner, however, said the term "mediatrix" can be used with more than one meaning. Another way of looking at it is to realize that "God in Jesus Christ has so established grace within the human community's solidarity in history and eternal welfare and loss, that it reaches one member through another, even though in God's perspective, it is intended equally directed for each, in Jesus Christ, head of the one human race. None of us produces grace, freshly causing something not yet there, bringing it into being. But we are intermediaries, and in this sense mediators of grace for each other." Even those who have gone before us on earth can be our mediators.[82] Rahner then applied this to Mary.

> When God looks upon the one community of the redeemed, and wills each with all the others and because he wills the others, he also looks upon this eternal Yes of the blessed Virgin, the Yes on which he willed, in this order of creation, the salvation of us all, quite directly and absolutely once and for all, to depend. God, therefore, wills our salvation too, in this view of his of Mary as she is in eternal life. When he looks upon her, he sees in her too only the grace of the Word made flesh, and he wills us on her account only because he loves her as the mother of his Son. But because God gives what is his sheer grace to its recipient in such a way that it is truly possessed as the recipient's own, though it still continues inalienably to belong to God and to Christ, this special and individual grace of God is only really recognized and praised when those to whom it is given are aware of it. Such praise does not diminish, but increases the glory of the utter grace of the one mediator. For that reason, there,

---

79. K. Rahner, *Mary the Mother of the Lord*, pp. 93-94.
80. K. Rahner, *Mary the Mother of the Lord*, p. 94.
81. K. Rahner, *Mary the Mother of the Lord*, p. 95.
82. K. Rahner, *Mary the Mother of the Lord*, p. 97.

we can truly say of Mary, on account of what she did in the history of redemption, which has become eternal, that in the communion of saints she is the intercessor for all of us, the mediatrix of all graces.[83]

One of Karl Rahner's famous contemporaries was **Hans Urs von Balthasar (1905-1988)**. Though his literary output was not as great as that of Rahner, nevertheless, it was considerable and not concentrated in one area. A good place to start is a short work he published a year before his death, *Mary for Today*.[84] He began by saying: "The best way to learn something about Mary and how she is related to our present age is to start with chapter 12 of Revelation. This question is at the core of this last book of the Bible, which uses visionary images to provide insight into the drama of the world's history."[85] Balthasar pointed out that in this book of the Bible "Mary becomes the Church," and that the "devil's rage against the Church is as great as it is because it is not able to achieve anything against her."[86] The woman fled into the desert, to a place prepared by God. Mary "in the hidden seclusion of her earthly life already experienced beforehand everything that her children would later encounter in the way of unpleasantness and consolation."[87] She lived in close contact with Jesus during his public life, and witnessed people's sometimes hostile reactions to him. Yet she stood by Jesus, not understanding everything people said about him. "She would not have done this if she did not know that the nature and fate of this young man were something unique and would be suitably revealed in the future."[88] The woman's children fought back against the powers of evil with no weapon but the "two-edged sword that issues from the mouth of God's Word. . . . But it should be noted that while the woman's children fight, the woman herself, though pursued, does not. . . . [The] woman, the Church as virgin who gives birth, cannot. For the whole period of the history of the world she is ensconced in the 'place prepared for her by God,' where she does not have to struggle for her keep but is 'nourished' by God."[89]

83. K. Rahner, *Mary the Mother of the Lord*, p. 101.
84. Hans Urs von Balthasar, *Mary for Today* (San Francisco: Ignatius Press, 1988).
85. Balthasar, *Mary for Today*, p. 9.
86. Balthasar, *Mary for Today*, p. 11.
87. Balthasar, *Mary for Today*, p. 14.
88. Balthasar, *Mary for Today*, p. 17.
89. Balthasar, *Mary for Today*, pp. 19-20.

Although Mary was preserved from original sin, she bore her son in pain. She stands in solidarity with Eve, the mother of the race, because she is free of sin. What she suffers is expiation for Eve and her descendants.[90] Although she remained a virgin, how "her womb opened and closed again we do not know, and it is superfluous to speculate about an event which for God was a child's game."[91] Virginity, such as Mary possessed, is a "conscious and free surrender of one's physical fertility, which nevertheless can only bring forth what is doomed to die, in order to share in the new fruitfulness of the Cross and Resurrection which is able to generate and bring to birth what is truly immortal."[92] "Mary as a virgin with her son gave birth to the last age, for she is the epitome and the embodiment of Israel, which awaited the birth-pangs of the Messiah as a sign that the final and definitive world had broken in on us."[93]

In a chapter titled "Mary, the Memory of the Church," Balthasar maintained that, although Mary did not know everything onward from the time that the angel first approached her,[94] she had grasped certain things such as that of her role as advocate (e.g., for the poor at the wedding feast at Cana),[95] and that she prayed together with the assembled Church for the Holy Spirit (Acts 1:14).[96] She is the teacher of the Church because in her we "recognize the depth of God's love in the work of his Incarnation and redemption."[97]

Balthasar treated marriage and virginity specifically in a chapter dedicated to those two topics. He highlighted the importance of marriage in Israel, but also noted that Jeremiah was forbidden to marry, Ezekiel lost his wife, and Hosea was married to a prostitute.[98] The marriage of Mary and Joseph was one in which the husband's married life "meant a renunciation on the basis of faith and at the same time a sharing in the virginal faithfulness of his wife." This marriage "is a model both for married people and for celibates in Christ's Church."[99] Marriage is a reflection of Christ's rela-

90. Balthasar, *Mary for Today,* p. 23.
91. Balthasar, *Mary for Today,* p. 25.
92. Balthasar, *Mary for Today,* p. 26.
93. Balthasar, *Mary for Today,* p. 29.
94. Balthasar, *Mary for Today,* p. 36.
95. Balthasar, *Mary for Today,* p. 38.
96. Balthasar, *Mary for Today,* p. 39.
97. Balthasar, *Mary for Today,* p. 42.
98. Balthasar, *Mary for Today,* pp. 49-52.
99. Balthasar, *Mary for Today,* pp. 52-53.

tionship to his Church. "'For as woman was made from man, so man is now born of woman' (1 Cor 11:12). In this statement the position of Mary — never prominent in Paul — is once again clear."[100]

In a papacy that lasted more than twenty-six years (1978-2005), **Pope John Paul II** "has left behind an enormous legacy. It includes more than seventy thousand pages of teaching found in encyclicals, apostolic exhortations and letters, homilies, letters, and other published texts. His teaching took up a wide range of themes — from the self-revelation of God, through the sacramental life of the church, relations with other Christians and the followers of other religions, to questions of social and sexual morality, and on to the basic elements in the Christian spiritual life."[101] Obviously the Pope had much to say about Mary.

The Pope spoke of Mary as the image of the heavenly Church,[102] showed that the Church has grown in her understanding of Mary's role,[103] stressed that Mary's mediation is derived from Christ and in no way overshadows it,[104] reaffirmed that Mary is the Virgin Mother of God,[105] and asserted that to honor Mary is to go to Jesus,[106] and so on. Such mentions of Mary in various talks show us how the Pope applied the teachings of Vatican II on Mary to concrete situations in people's lives.

The Pope also wrote sixteen encyclicals. One written in 1987 is titled *Redemptoris Mater (On the Blessed Virgin Mary in the Life of the Pilgrim Church).*[107] This document was more devotional than Pope Paul VI's earlier document, *Marialis Cultus* (1974), since it was used to introduce the "Year of Mary." In this post–Vatican II document the Pope saluted Mary as the Church's own beginning, "for in the event of the Immaculate Conception the Church sees projected, and anticipated in her most noble member, the saving grace of Easter." He also recalled the letters of his predecessor, Pope Paul VI, on the special veneration the Mother of God receives in the

---

100. Balthasar, *Mary for Today,* pp. 55-56.

101. Gerald O'Collins, Daniel Kendall, and Jeffrey LaBelle, eds., *Pope John Paul II: A Reader* (New York/Mahwah, NJ: Paulist, 2007), p. vii.

102. A July 4, 1999, talk at the dedication of a Shrine of Divine Love near Rome.

103. November 8, 1995, at a General Audience.

104. General Audience on October 1, 1997.

105. General Audience on September 13, 1995.

106. General Audience on November 15, 1995.

107. "Redemptoris Mater," in J. Michael Miller's *The Encyclicals of John Paul II* (Huntington, IN: Our Sunday Visitor, 2001).

Church, as well as various forms of Marian devotion. John Paul II believed that as we celebrated the jubilee year of 2000, we needed to "precede that anniversary by a similar Jubilee in celebration of the birth of Mary."[108] He emphasized that the "Second Vatican Council, by presenting Mary in the mystery of Christ, also finds the path to a deeper understanding of the mystery of the Church. Mary, as the Mother of Christ, is in a particular way united with the Church, 'which the Lord established as his own body.'" Mary is the model of the Church, who has gone before us, and is both mother and virgin.[109] At the annunciation by the angel, Mary was introduced into the mystery of Christ.[110] She was preserved from the inheritance of original sin, and received life from him to whom she herself gave life.[111]

The Pope spent a large part of the encyclical on Mary's faith,[112] and her role as mother.[113] The Pope also spoke of Mary as the Mother of the Pilgrim Church.[114] Finally, the Pope addressed Mary's "Maternal Mediation."[115] Obviously he agreed with St. Paul that there is only one mediator between God and us (Christ Jesus), but because of her cooperation in God's divine plan and her cooperation with her Son's whole mission and her Son himself, her cooperation was "precisely this mediation subordinated to the mediation of Christ."[116] "Through her mediation, subordinate to that of the Redeemer, Mary contributes in a special way to the union of the pilgrim Church on earth with the eschatological and heavenly reality of the Communion of Saints, since she has already been 'assumed into heaven.'"[117] She is "a figure of the Church in the matter of faith, charity, and perfect union with Christ."[118]

In 1992 Pope John Paul II promulgated the *Catechism of the Catholic Church*. In the document accompanying the 1997 edition he said that peo-

108. "Redemptoris Mater," p. 319.
109. "Redemptoris Mater," p. 321.
110. "Redemptoris Mater," p. 323.
111. "Redemptoris Mater," p. 325.
112. "Redemptoris Mater," pp. 326-33.
113. "Redemptoris Mater," pp. 333-49.
114. "Redemptoris Mater," pp. 338-49.
115. "Redemptoris Mater," pp. 349-63.
116. "Redemptoris Mater," p. 351.
117. "Redemptoris Mater," pp. 352-53.
118. "Redemptoris Mater," p. 354.

ple "will find in this genuine, systematic presentation of the faith and of Catholic doctrine a totally reliable way to present, with renewed fervor, each and every part of the Christian message to the people of our time."[119]

The *Catechism* is divided into four parts: (1) the Profession of Faith (Creed); (2) Celebration of the Christian Mystery (Church and Sacraments); (3) Life in Christ (morality); and (4) Christian Prayer. Mary is treated under the Profession of Faith, specifically under two phrases: "[Jesus] was conceived by the power of the Holy Spirit and born of the Virgin Mary," and "I believe in the Holy Catholic Church." Here the *Catechism* reflects Vatican II in considering Mary in light of the mystery of Christ and that of the Church. It mentions that "Mary's role in the Church is inseparable from her union with Christ and flows directly from it" (964); after her Son's Ascension, Mary "aided the beginnings of the Church by her prayers" (965); the "Immaculate Virgin, preserved free from all stain of original sin, when the course of her earthly life was finished, was taken up body and soul into heavenly glory" (966); the "Virgin Mary is the Church's model of faith and charity. Thus she is a 'preeminent and . . . wholly unique member of the Church'" (967); "she is a mother to us in the order of grace" (968). The Church rightly honors "the Blessed Virgin with special devotion. From the most ancient times the Blessed Virgin has been honored with the title of 'Mother of God'" (971). "In her we contemplate what the Church already is in her mystery on her own 'pilgrimage of faith,' and what she will be in the homeland at the end of her journey" (972).

One very interesting trend to observe is the growing diversity *within* liberation theology, to which we now turn. Liberation theology, of course, is a very broad terrain to map, moving geographically from Latin America to North America to Europe, Asia, and Africa, and moving sociologically from Latin American to African American to African to Feminist to Womanist to Queer. In the light of this diversity, perhaps it is wiser to speak of liberation theologies. Perhaps the only themes uniting such diverse groups of Christian thinkers is that theology is invariably contextual and that they are self-consciously engaging in theology from within the context of a socially marginalized group. It is perhaps natural,

---

119. Apostolic Letter of Pope John Paul II, *Laetamur Magnopere* (August 15, 1997), which accompanied the promulgation of the second edition. The subsequent citations are from the second (1997) edition (Vatican City: Libreria Editrice Vatican; Washington, DC: [distributed by] United States Catholic Conference, 2000).

within such a discussion, to begin with feminist theologians and with a true classic in the field, **Rosemary Radford Ruether**'s essay, "Mistress of Heaven: The Meaning of Mariology."[120] Ruether rejects in the strongest possible language the "Mary of the monks," as a feminine ideal not only created and idolized by men, but also harmful and impossible for real women to emulate. She is harmful insofar as she embodies passivity, silence, and obedience as the proper female responses to suffering and justice, and impossible insofar as she idealizes both virginity and motherhood while denigrating (especially female) sexuality. So damaged is the mother of Jesus by centuries of male hierarchy, and so damaging is she to Christian women, that as a liberative symbol she is irredeemable. The solution Ruether proposes is therefore to baptize the Great Mother pre-Christian traditions by infusing them into another symbolic Mary — the Magdalene.[121]

Perhaps unsurprisingly, the three decades since the publication of this essay have not seen a wide transference of devotional loyalty from the mother of Jesus to the first witness to the resurrection, whether by women or men. Ruether herself seemed to back away from the proposal in 1983, when, in *Sexism and God-Talk,* she offered a powerful reading of the Magnificat to ground a liberation Mariology.[122] Perhaps Mary as symbol can be reimagined after all. There is, of course, no agreement as to what such reimagination might look like. To plot the extremes, we offer two examples: **Elizabeth Johnson** and **Tina Beattie.** At one end of the spectrum, Johnson hopes to reinvigorate feminist Catholic thinking about Mary through a close reading of the biblical texts. The result is a theologically minimal though biblically rich Mary (though Johnson is very careful not to deny any of the Marian dogmas) with whom Protestants would be familiar and who could serve as a model disciple across boundaries created by sex/gender and confession.[123] At the other end, Beattie proposes a liberating understanding of Mary, not by attenuating the tradition, but by at-

---

120. Rosemary Radford Ruether, "Mistress of Heaven: The Meaning of Mariology," in *New Woman, New Earth: Sexist Ideologies and Human Liberation* (New York: Seabury, 1975), pp. 36-62.

121. Ruether, "Mistress of Heaven," p. 59.

122. Rosemary Radford Ruether, *Sexism and God-Talk* (Boston: Beacon, 1983), pp. 139-58.

123. Elizabeth Johnson, *Truly Our Sister: A Theology of Mary in the Communion of Saints* (New York: Continuum, 2004).

tending to overlooked scraps of the patristic tradition and using these to push that tradition to its logical and theological, gynocentric conclusions. The goal is no less than the institution of a female Marian priesthood that would finally overturn the patriarchal association of women's bodies with impurity and death without also rejecting accepted Church teaching on sexual difference.[124]

The tension between Marian minimalism and maximalism is mirrored in other kinds of Catholic liberation and postcolonial theology. Paralleling Johnson's feminist minimalism is that of Sri Lankan theologian **Tissa Balasuriya** in his work, *Mary and Human Liberation*.[125] Balasuriya — like Johnson above — emphasizes Mary's courage and cooperation with Jesus throughout her life, even as a widow. And, like Johnson, Balasuriya pushes the traditional Marian dogmas into the background because he perceives them to have removed Mary from the life-experiences of the world's poor and marginalized, a disproportionate number of whom are women and children. Balasuriya insists that what matters about Mary is "not so much that she is immaculate, a virgin, and in what form she is mother of God, but that she was intimately associated with Jesus of Nazareth, flesh of her flesh, in the beginning of the new community. This new community was to carry the message of human liberation. . . . In this, Mary is an example to all humankind."[126] She prophetically discloses the Church's preferential option for the poor in her Magnificat and, for Balasuriya, any dogma that blurs this disclosure is to be set aside. Balasuriya's construction of an either/or argument coupled with a popular and imprecise style brought him into conflict with his superiors and led eventually to his 1997 excommunication from the Roman Catholic Church.[127] The excommunication was rescinded one year later.

At the other extreme, **Leonardo Boff**'s maximal presentation in *The Maternal Face of God*[128] has been understood by critics both Catholic and

124. Tina Beattie, *God's Mother, Eve's Advocate: A Marian Narrative of Women's Salvation* (New York: Continuum, 2002).

125. Tissa Balasuriya, OMI, *Mary and Human Liberation: The Story and the Text*, ed. Helen Stanton (Harrisburg, PA: Trinity Press International, 1997).

126. Balasuriya, *Mary and Human Liberation*, pp. 77-78.

127. See Edmund Hill, OP, "The Balasuriya File," in Stanton, ed., *Mary and Human Liberation*, pp. 1-12.

128. Leonardo Boff, *The Maternal Face of God: The Feminine and Its Religious Expression*, trans. Robert Barr and John Dierksmeier (Maryknoll, NY: Orbis, 1987).

Protestant as approaching and even crossing the line of heresy. On the one hand, it seems as though Boff wishes to construct a Latin American liberation Mariology similar to Balasuriya's. In the chapter, "Mary, Prophetic Woman of Liberation," he attends to the foundational experiences of oppression, violence, and especially crippling poverty among local faith communities and how these, in turn, have shaped their understanding of the Mother of Jesus. He observes that while traditional Mariology has paid little attention to the Magnificat, the poor of Latin America are transfixed by its prophetic denunciation of the powerful and declaration of God's favor toward the weak. On the other hand, he radically hypothesizes "that the Virgin Mary, Mother of God and of all men and women, realizes the feminine absolutely and eschatologically, inasmuch as the Holy Spirit has made her his temple, sanctuary, and tabernacle in so real and genuine a way that she is to be regarded as hypostatically united to the Third Person of the Blessed Trinity."[129] The result is a very high Mariology in which immaculate conception, virginal maternity, and bodily assumption are supplemented with very strong notions of co-redemption and co-mediation. For, as the incarnation of the Holy Spirit, Boff's Mary is Christ's equal. At no point does Boff attempt to harmonize this hypostatic expression of silence and repose with the active and prophetic Mary who sang the Magnificat.

## Modern Protestant Thought

On the Protestant side, the five centuries following the Reformation have been marked largely by a trend from minimalism to silence. It is only in the last half of the twentieth century that Protestant theologians have turned again to reflect on Mary and, strikingly, for reasons very similar to those of the Fathers — have done so in order better to understand and in some ways to reclaim the full teaching of the Church on the identity of the incarnate Lord. Thus, in the classic sixteenth-century confessions Mary is a minor theme at best. Despite its founder's unquestioned Marian devotion and sentimentality, Mary is unmentioned in the Lutheran *Augsburg Confession* (1530), at best included only by inference in Article 21, which forbids the invocation of saints.[130] The *Formula of Concord* (1576) amplifies this posi-

---

129. Boff, *The Maternal Face of God*, p. 93.
130. *The Augsburg Confession*, Art. 21, in Philip Schaff, ed., *The Creeds of Christendom*,

tion only slightly to defend the reality of Mary's motherhood and the propriety of the title, Mother of God.[131] Among the Reformed, the approach is similar. Earlier documents such as the *Heidelberg Catechism* (1563) and the *Second Helvetic Confession* (1566) mention her with reference to the Incarnation (the latter includes the modifier *semper virgine* [ever-virgin]),[132] thereby establishing a trend from which the later *Westminster Confession of Faith* (1647) does not depart.[133] The same minimalism is found in the dogmatics of the time.[134] Apart from a necessary nod to secure the full humanity of the Incarnate Lord, Mary was largely regarded at best as superfluous and at worst as the personification of major Reformation debates and a source of harmful superstitious pious practice.

Of course, once the traditional language used to express the identity of Jesus was called into question, she became redundant in Protestant dogmatics altogether. Although the case can be made that this move began in the transition to a Christology of function embodied in Melanchthon's dictum, "to know Christ is to know his benefits," the modern questions arose from two sources. First, higher biblical criticism, whose methodologies and conclusions appeared to undermine notions of scriptural inerrancy and inspiration, eroded the theological epistemology common in the Protestant dogmatic systems of the seventeenth and eighteenth centuries and accordingly, the confidence with which the Protestant rationalists could engage in apologetics against Enlightenment criticism of Christian faith. Second, the advent of the Romantic movement from approximately 1780 onwards seemed to suggest that profound religious engagement with the world could take place apart from institutional religious (i.e., Christian) commitment and, indeed, could be all the richer when separated from it. **Friedrich Schleiermacher (1763-1834)** sought to engage both trends apologetically by

---

vol. 3, *The Evangelical Protestant Creeds with Translations*, 4th ed. (New York: Harper & Brothers, 1919), p. 26.

131. *The Formula of Concord*, 8.6-7, and 12.1, in *Creeds of Christendom*, 3: 150, 174.

132. See *The Heidelberg Catechism*, q. 35, in *Creeds of Christendom*, 3: 319; and *The Second Helvetic Confession* 10.4, in *Creeds of Christendom*, 3: 255.

133. *The Westminster Confession of Faith* 8.2, in *Creeds of Christendom*, 3: 619.

134. See, e.g., the extensive summaries found in Heinrich Heppe, *Reformed Dogmatics: Set Out and Illustrated from the Sources*, rev. and ed. Ernst Bizer, trans. G. T. Thomson (Grand Rapids: Baker, 1978), pp. 421-28, 444; and Heinrich Schmid, *The Doctrinal Theology of the Evangelical Lutheran Church*, 3rd ed., trans. Charles A. Hay and Henry E. Jacobs (Minneapolis: Augsburg, 1899), pp. 293-309.

arguing that an intellectually robust and experientially profound Christian commitment not only withstood critical and romantic questioning, but even incorporated their findings. This approach is clearly on display in his treatment of miracles. Where the "cultured despiser" of Christianity mocks its miracles, Schleiermacher argues that miracles are irrelevant to faith. Whereas once, the miraculous may have evoked and/or confirmed recognition of Christ, he never presented them as bases for faith.[135] Faith and reason need not conflict, for miracles are not necessary. "What takes the place of miracles for our time is our historical knowledge of the character, as well as of the scope and the duration, of Christ's spiritual achievements."[136] Mary is implicated in this discussion because, of course, the Virgin Birth of Christ is just such a miracle. Accordingly, Schleiermacher contends that although its affirmation does not denigrate the faith, its denial does not challenge belief in Christ as the Redeemer;[137] it has, therefore, no dogmatic value.[138] Accordingly, traditional beliefs that have evolved from this doctrine (namely, those regarding Mary's virginity and purity) are similarly superfluous.[139] In Schleiermacher's view, dogmatic Marian reflection is part and parcel of an earlier age, now no longer necessary.

As a result of Schleiermacher's stature, Marian silence in Protestant dogmatics prevailed for over a century. It was not until **Karl Barth (1886-1968)** boldly returned Mary to the forefront of the dogmatic enterprise that, in combination to the openness signaled in the Second Vatican Council, the situation began to change. Barth's approach to Mary is threefold: (1) a defense not only of the propriety but indeed the Christological necessity of *Theotokos*; (2) a pungent rejection of any attempt to decouple Marian reflection from Christology; and (3) an exposition of the miracle of the Virgin Birth in which Mary expresses the dilemma of humanity at large. Turning first to (1), Barth insists that "it amounts to a test of the proper understanding of the incarnation of the Word, that as Christians and theologians we do not reject the description of Mary as the 'mother of God,' but in spite of its being overloaded by the so-called Mariology of the

---

135. Friedrich Schleiermacher, *The Christian Faith*, 2nd ed., trans. H. R. Mackintosh and J. S. Stewart (Edinburgh: T. & T. Clark, 1928), p. 448.

136. Schleiermacher, *The Christian Faith*. He therefore concludes that belief in miracles "belongs not so much to our faith in Christ directly as to our faith in Scripture" (p. 449).

137. Schleiermacher, *The Christian Faith*, pp. 403-4.

138. Schleiermacher, *The Christian Faith*, p. 404.

139. Schleiermacher, *The Christian Faith*, p. 405.

Roman Catholic Church, we affirm and approve of it as a legitimate development of christological truth."[140] It is for the sake of a right understanding of the person and work of Jesus Christ — and, Barth would add, consequently everything else — that the term needs to be taken up again. However necessary, though, Barth is clear that this move is risky.

Turning to (2), Barth stresses — this time negatively — that the ground on which Marian reflection is legitimately to take place is Christology. Here, it is worth quoting him at length:

> [Deploying "Mother of God"] as the basis of an independent Mariology (as it is called) was and is one of those characteristically Roman Catholic enterprises against which there has to be an Evangelical protest not only for their arbitrariness in form but also for the precariousness of their content. . . . Nor can we conclude otherwise from the most earnest interpretations of the dogma which have arisen than that in this case we are dealing essentially, not with an illumination, but with an obscuring of revealed truth, in other words, with a false doctrine.[141]

As a theological locus independent of Christology, Mariology is roundly condemned because it gives rise to forms of devotion to one other than the One disclosed in Jesus Christ. It is important to note, however, that Barth does not thus charge his Catholic opponents with the deification of Mary, as was and remains fairly commonplace in popular Protestant polemics. The devotion is not to Mary-as-goddess, but to Mary-as-exalted-creature; and the heresy (for that is the word he uses) such devotion expresses is that there is a point of contact outside that established by God in the union of divinity and humanity in Jesus Christ, a point of contact from which human beings, as exemplified in Mary, can move toward God. In short, Mariology betrays a belief that Jesus Christ does not save, but rather helps us to save ourselves. And Barth will have none of it.

Is there then any room for constructive Marian remarks? As we move to (3), given the sharpness of Barth's previous language, readers might be surprised to discover that the answer is in fact yes. For the core of Barth's objection to Catholic Mariology is not whether Mary exemplifies human-

---

140. Karl Barth, *CD* I/2, p. 138; see also *CD* IV/2, p. 71.
141. *CD* I/2, p. 139.

ity at large, but how she does so. It is his deep conviction that Mary, rightly understood within the bounds of Christology, displays not a natural receptivity to grace, but a natural incapacity to God's gift which is taken up in the power of the Spirit and transformed. If the reality of her motherhood is a sign pointing to the identity of the One conceived in her womb, her virginity explicitly points to the fact that in itself, human nature is utterly incapable of becoming the human nature of God the Son.[142] It functions as a sign that human beings must be first graciously transformed and only then respond in faith to the gracious gift of God's saving self-disclosure in Jesus Christ. Upon "this human nature a mystery must be wrought in order that this may be made possible. And this mystery must consist in its receiving the capacity for God which it does not possess. This mystery is signified by the *natus ex virgine.*"[143] With Barth, then, Mary is back on the Protestant dogmatic agenda.[144]

142. *CD* I/2, p. 187. See also *CD* II/1, p. 540. Barth later elaborates in this way: "man is involved in the form of Mary, but involved only in the form of the *virgo Maria,* i.e., only in the form of non-willing, non-achieving, non-creative, non-sovereign man, only in the form of man who can merely receive, merely be ready, merely let something be done to and with himself. This human being, the *virgo,* becomes the possibility, becomes the mother of God's Son in the flesh. It is not, of course, that she is this; but she becomes it. And she does not become it of her own capacity; she acquires capacity by the act of the Son of God assuming flesh" (*CD* I/2, p. 191). This theme, of course, is found in Barth's early work (see *CD* I/1, pp. 485-86) and his later work, as in *The Faith of the Church: A Commentary on the Apostles' Creed according to Calvin's Catechism,* trans. Gabriel Vahanian (London: Fontana, 1958), pp. 72-74; *Credo* (New York: Scribner's, 1962), pp. 62-72.

143. *CD* I/2, pp. 188-89. Barth continues, "It is not, then, as if at this point a door is opened which can lead to Mariology and thus to a doctrine of the goodness of the creature and its capacity for God, to a doctrine of the independent holiness of the Church. This only can and must be said here: in the form of this act of divine justification and sanctification, and so in the mystery of the divine mercy, human nature (apart from sinful human history and in spite of the corruption proper to human nature itself), is made worthy to be a partaker of the divine nature by grace and by a miracle of grace. In token of that the woman is adopted apart from the male and her relation to him, and in spite of the sin of which she is guilty along with him, to be conceiver of the eternal God Himself on earth, to be the Θεοτόκος" (*CD* I/2, p. 196). In *CD* IV/2, p. 45, he summarizes the same theme in this way: Humankind "is not the guarantor of His being. It was only there when He became — in the form of the people Israel, which was itself elected without its own co-operation or merit, and concretely in the form of Mary, who concludes the history of this people. It was not, however, Israel or Mary who acted, but God — acting towards Israel and finally . . . towards Mary. In all these forms man was and is only admitted and adopted into unity with the Son of God."

144. One of Barth's critics has insisted that the move puts him on the road toward Ro-

No one in mainstream North American Protestant theology has done more to press this conclusion than Lutheran theologian **Robert W. Jenson**. With Barth, he anchors Marian discussion within Christology, insisting that Jesus "from *Mary's womb* to the Ascension" is the narrative content of God's self-introduction to human beings.[145] Accordingly, in a manner similar to Barth, Jenson defends the title *Theotokos* as a Christological necessity; a proper understanding of the identity of Jesus Christ as God Incarnate is impossible without it.[146] He is, however, prepared to go much farther than Barth in his declaration that Mary's pregnancy is rightly to be understood as a prophetic utterance[147] and that as a result, Mary is to be understood as the "archprophet" and "Israel in one person."[148] As such, she is asymmetrically related to the Church as the "member of the church who is what the church is to be, a 'type' of the church's essential character."[149] As the embodiment of the church's prophetic reality, she is to be called upon by Christians — not to speak God's word to us (she has done that already), but to speak God's word to God on believers' behalf.[150] On the modern dogmas of Immaculate Conception and Bodily Assumption, Jenson is even more provocative. He acknowledges the difficulty that many Christians have with the notion of *sinlessness,* and attempts a redefinition thereof as faithfulness to her vocation first expressed in her *fiat mihi* and continued throughout her life thereafter. On this reading, the modern Marian doctrines are simply to be inferred from a reading of Mary's place in Matthew 1–2 into where she would naturally fit in John 1. When such a task is undertaken, Immaculate Conception and Bodily Assumption "immediately result,"[151] even if Jenson

---

man Catholic "Mariology" and even "Mariolatry." See Wolfhart Pannenberg, *Jesus — God and Man,* trans. Lewis L. Wilkins and Duane A. Priebe (London: SCM, 1968), pp. 144-47. Pannenberg thoroughly rejects the move himself, arguing that the Gospel account of the miraculous virginal conception and subsequent theological reflection thereon is inconsistent with the Christologies of John and Paul.

145. Robert W. Jenson, *The Works of God,* vol. 2 of his *Systematic Theology* (New York: Oxford University Press, 1999), p. 61.

146. Robert W. Jenson, *The Triune God,* vol. 1 of his *Systematic Theology* (New York: Oxford University Press, 1997), pp. 127-29.

147. Jenson, *The Works of God,* p. 198.

148. Robert W. Jenson, "A Space for God," in *Mary, Mother of God,* ed. Carl E. Braaten and Robert W. Jenson (Grand Rapids: Eerdmans, 2004), pp. 49-57, quotations from p. 56.

149. Jenson, *The Works of God,* p. 202.

150. Jenson, *The Works of God,* pp. 202-3.

151. Jenson, *The Works of God,* p. 204.

frankly finds the definition of the second dogma to be obtuse and perhaps intellectually vacuous. Clearly, very few Protestant theologians are willing to pursue such maximal readings of the Marian tradition. Nevertheless, Mary continues to be a subject for discussion and debate in a variety of theological arenas.

The renewed interest in and diversity among Marian studies has, since the Second Vatican Council, also led to very interesting developments in cross-confessional dialogues. The following deserve particular mention. In the latter part of the twentieth century, the U.S. **Lutheran-Catholic Dialogue** published a collection of fifteen essays and a common statement of convergences and divergences regarding Mary as she was understood in relation to Christ and in relation to the communion of saints.[152] In Europe, meanwhile, the **Groupe des Dombes** — a private association of French-speaking Lutheran, Reformed, and Roman Catholic theologians — published a twofold study of Mary, calling for a "conversion of the churches" in which Protestants and Catholics together would begin to consider whether their differences regarding Mary are truly church dividing.[153] Most recently, these documents have been joined by a third, *Mary: Grace and Hope in Christ*, the Agreed Statement by the **Anglican–Roman Catholic International Commission (ARCIC)**.[154] The document seeks to sketch in broad strokes just how far Anglicans and Catholics might be able to journey together in the Marian affirmations while remaining true to their own traditions. In the Anglican Communion, given the spectrum of theological views it contains, the document's reception has been mixed at best.[155] Finally, the American group **Evangelicals and Catholics Together** released a document titled "Do Whatever He Tells You: The Place of the

---

152. G. Anderson et al., eds., *The One Mediator, the Saints, and Mary*, Lutherans and Catholics in Dialogue 8 (Minneapolis: Fortress, 1992).

153. Alain Blancy, Maurice Jourjon, and the Groupe des Dombes, *Mary in the Plan of God and in the Communion of Saints* (New York: Paulist, 2002). First published as *Marie dans le dessein de Dieu et la communion des saints* (Paris: Bayard, 1999).

154. Donald Bolen and Gregory Cameron, eds., *Mary: Grace and Hope in Christ: The Text with Commentaries and Study Guide* (New York: Continuum, 2006). The preparatory papers have also been published as Adelbert Denaux and Nicholas Sagovsky, eds., *Studying Mary: The Virgin Mary in Anglican and Roman Catholic Theology and Devotion*, The ARCIC Working Papers (Edinburgh: T. & T. Clark, 2007).

155. See, for an especially nuanced example of such reception, the analysis of Fulcrum, an evangelical group within the Church of England, available at http://www.fulcrum-anglican .org.uk/news/2005/20050528arcicmary.cfm?doc=40.

Blessed Virgin Mary in Christian Faith and Life" late in 2009.[156] As with the ARCIC declaration, it is safe to say that the reactions to this document will range widely, from the optimistic through the cautious to the caustic.

Modern Protestant thought about Mary, then, can be plotted along a parabola, with the early confessions and Protestant rationalists speaking of her within strongly Christological parameters, slowly descending into silence. Later these parameters gave way under the advent of liberal Protestant thought, and began to ascend in the work of Barth and finally, to flower with Jenson and various dialogical documents.

## Modern Orthodoxy

It might strike some readers as odd that, until now, nothing has been written about the place of Mary in the doctrine and devotion of the churches of the East. Some might wonder whether this silence has reflected the expertise of the authors — one Anglican, one Roman Catholic, both Latin. While this no doubt has had an influence on the content so far presented, it is not quite fair to use it as a reason for neglecting Orthodoxy. On the contrary, I (Tim) would argue that Orthodoxy has not been neglected at all, for the history of mariological development up to 431 and the dogmatic definition of *Theotokos* at the Council of Ephesus simply *is* the history of Mary in Orthodoxy. Dogmatically, Marian reflection in Eastern Christianity reached its climax in the victory of St. Cyril of Alexandria.

The dogmatic material that follows Ephesus in our narrative — the adoption and development of St. Augustine's doctrine of Original Sin, the development of the doctrine and then dogma of the Immaculate Conception, and the definition of the Bodily Assumption as dogma are peculiarly Western, and that has inevitably narrowed our focus. And yet, more needs to be said. For even if dogmatic definitions ceased in 431, Marian reflection and devotion continue to be a part of the living tradition of Eastern Christianity that is passed on from one generation to the next. This short section therefore highlights Orthodox challenges to the modern dogmas and briefly presents the place of the most holy *Theotokos* in Orthodox liturgy.

The Orthodox have rejected the Roman Catholic dogmatic definitions

---

156. Private email from Fr. Richard John Neuhaus to Tim Perry, Friday, November 14, 2008.

of the Immaculate Conception (1854) and the Bodily Assumption (1950) for four reasons. The first two have to do with the manner of their promulgation. First, the Orthodox object to the singular role played by the Pope in the dogmas' definitions. They challenge the notion that the Pope may act alone in defining articles of faith as dogma. While it is certainly true that both Pius IX and Pius XII consulted widely before issuing their respective bulls, the final definition was pronounced on the basis of their own unique magisterial authority as the successors of St. Peter. The Orthodox challenge the notion that such authority exists. Similarly, these pronouncements resulted from nonconciliar processes and were not themselves products of a Council; therefore, according to the Orthodox they cannot be universally binding. These, of course, are modern applications of the traditional Orthodox criticisms of the Western understandings of the papal office and the place and purpose of the Councils of the Church, objections that are as old as the Great Schism of 1054.

The remaining Orthodox objections have more to do with the dogmas' contents. For the Orthodox, third, the dogmas are, strictly speaking, unnecessary. Dogmatic definitions are necessitated by the challenges of heresy. Nicea was occasioned by Arianism, Constantinople by Pneumatomachianism, Ephesus by Nestorianism, Chalcedon by Eutychianism, etc. In the Orthodox mind, there was no heretical teaching concerning Mary's purity or heavenly abode that needed correcting. Therefore, even if true — and certainly there is no dispute within Orthodoxy concerning the Bodily Assumption — these decrees are at best superfluous. Finally, fourth, both dogmatic decrees, and the dogma of the Immaculate Conception particularly, are regarded by most Orthodox to be tainted by an unbiblical and untraditional (i.e., Augustinian) doctrine of Original Sin. From an Orthodox point of view, a defective view of human nature underlies and undermines the dogmas.[157]

The shared suspicion towards Augustine, however, is no guarantee that Orthodox teaching regarding Mary's purity is uniform. **Alexander Lebedev**, a Russian Orthodox theologian writing in the nineteenth century, expresses an Orthodox position that might be said to be classical. Mary, he believes, inherited the corrupted human nature of Adam — that

---

157. The four objections are helpfully set forth in Emmanuel Lanne, OSB, "Marian Issues from an Eastern Perspective," in Denaux and Sagovsky, eds., *Studying Mary,* pp. 60-72, esp. 62-63.

is, a nature rendered subject to death by Adam's sin, but one nevertheless able to cooperate with grace. This nature was then sanctified by God prior to Mary's birth, just as was the humanity of the prophet Jeremiah and John the Baptist. Mary was further rendered immaculate through her constant cooperation with God's grace, a cooperation that achieved its apex at Golgotha.[158] Within this broad position, however, there is room for considerable diversity. At a maximalist end, we find the view of **Sergei Bulgakov**, who disputes the notion that "immaculacy" is a privilege extended to Mary in the light of the redemption that would be won by her Son, as the Immaculate Conception is defined for Roman Catholics. For him, Mary's pure humanity is no less than the resurgence of unfallen creation. Though he insists that Mary is saved by Christ, his argument has generated some controversy within Orthodox circles.[159] The minimalist end is well represented by **Alexis Kniazeff**, who argues that the Feast of the Conception of Mary, from which the Latin dogma evolved in the medieval era, celebrates no more than Mary's prebirth sanctification in a manner similar to Jeremiah and John. Her immaculacy, he says, is better associated with her perpetual virginity, and its emphasis on obedience, than with some privilege given from the instant of her conception.[160] For it has to do with the fact that, throughout her life, in and through her continuous cooperation with grace, Mary never sinned. **John Meyendorff** acknowledges that even Augustinian doctrines of Original Sin and Immaculate Conception can sometimes be found among a minority of Orthodox theologians. In Meyendorff's view, such views do not represent authentic Orthodox doctrine, but have departed from the Fathers.[161]

Thus, Marian teaching in Orthodoxy may legitimately be said to be more minimal and more diverse than what is found in Catholicism. This is not to say, however, that Protestants will find handy allies in the Orthodox when it comes to critical engagements with Mariology.[162] For Mary's place

158. Quoted in Martin Jugie, *L'Imaculée Conception dans l'Écriture sainte et dans la tradition orientale* (Rome: Academia Mariana/Officium Libri Catholici, 1952), p. 448.

159. Sergei Bulgakov, *The Burning Bush: On the Orthodox Veneration of the Mother of God* (Grand Rapids: Eerdmans, 2009).

160. Alexis Kniazeff, *La Mère de Dieu dans L'Église Orthodoxe* (Paris: Cerf, 1990).

161. John Meyendorff, *Byzantine Theology: Historical Trends and Doctrinal Themes* (London: Mowbray, 1975), p. 144.

162. Lanne recounts how two early Lutheran theologians, David Chytraeus and Stephan Gerlach, approached the Orthodox with such a common critical project in mind

in the Orthodox liturgy[163] is more exalted than in the West. In Orthodox liturgy, Mary's intercessions are requested at the beginning and end of services, in ways far more elaborate than in any official Western liturgy. She is even said to "save" (though she is never called "Savior"). Furthermore, precisely because she shares in the fallen humanity of Adam, her constant cooperation with grace can be held up as the example of holiness to which all Christians can and should aspire, and especially for Christian ascetics. In a way foreign to Western Christian theological thought, Mary both shares our fallen nature and is exalted to a place higher than the cherubim and seraphim in heaven.

---

only to come away having concluded that, when it came to Mary, the Christian East needed to be reformed even more than the Romans (Lanne, "Marian Issues," p. 61).

163. The use of "liturgy" is deliberate. We are speaking of authorized forms of corporate worship, which is the lifeblood of Orthodox theology, not matters of popular or private piety, where diversity of the sublime and the strange can be expected, as in all forms of Christian expression.

# 4. Concluding Observations

### Daniel Kendall, SJ

How does all this translate into day-to-day life in the twenty-first century? Gerald O'Collins and Mario Farrugia connected people's devotion to Mary to their commitment to Christ. Usually Catholics display a crucifix rather than an empty cross. "They want to see his body and his wounds. This instinct has also prompted them into erecting in different parts of the world wayside scenes of Calvary. At the foot of the cross Christ's Mother often keeps her lonely vigil."[1] Catholics are also accustomed to seeing images of Mary standing by her dying Son or holding the newborn baby in her arms. Sometimes Christ does not directly appear (e.g., scenes of the Annunciation), but his presence is implied. Likewise prayers move from Mary to her Son, as in the Rosary. Even in Verdi's opera *The Force of Destiny*, Leonora asks the Virgin to intercede and secure her pardon and protection.

At the beginning of the Reformation, Erasmus (1466-1536) noted some of the flawed devotions to Mary, especially those that marginalized Christ and distorted her role in their petitionary prayers. Yet prayers and hymns have come out of the medieval period and remain with us today. Some of the hymns included *Salve Regina* ("Hail, Holy Queen") and *Alma Redemptoris Mater* ("Kind Mother of the Redeemer"), while composers such as Brahms, Dvořák, Schubert, Vivaldi, Verdi, and Palestrina used

---

1. Gerald O'Collins and Mario Farrugia, *Catholicism: The Story of Catholic Christianity* (Oxford: Oxford University Press, 2003), p. 369.

Mary as a theme of their compositions. We can truly say that a characteristic of the Catholic Church is that it is centered on Jesus Christ, along with Mary, his mother.[2]

The same point was made by Richard McBrien in his book *Catholicism*.[3] In his introduction to the section titled "Mary and the Saints," he said: "No theological and doctrinal presentation of Catholicism could claim to be at once comprehensive and complete, i.e., 'catholic,' if it were to leave out the Blessed Virgin Mary and the other saints."[4]

McBrien considered how Mary appears in the New Testament. He noted that she is treated almost exclusively in the Gospels and Acts of the Apostles, and that the comments she receives vary from the negative in Mark to the positive in Luke. In John's Gospel she becomes a symbol for other Christians. She is perhaps referenced secondarily in Revelation 12. Scripture alone does not solve the problem of whether she remained a virgin after the birth of Jesus.[5] In fact, there is "no second-century evidence of belief in Mary's remaining a virgin after the birth of Jesus *(post partum)*, apart from the implications of the *Protevangelium* [a noncanonical work]."[6]

McBrien saw a change occur, however, from the third century to the Middle Ages. He said: "Mary's perpetual virginity . . . came to be almost universally accepted from the third century on. . . . Both Latin and Greek writers saw in her the model of all virtues, in fact."[7] Factors contributing to this point of view were the Nestorian controversy and the Council of Ephesus. During this period feasts such as the Assumption, the Annunciation, and the Nativity of Mary were being added to the Church calendar. "Faith in Mary's power of intercession with God received a strong push from the growing belief in her assumption."[8]

During the Middle Ages Mary began to be seen as the redemptrix of captives, as the refuge of sinners, and as mediatrix between God and humans. Marian theology slowly began to be divorced from the Bible. Bernard of Clairvaux (1090-1153) did not deny that Christ was the one true

2. O'Collins and Farrugia, *Catholicism,* pp. 370-72.
3. Richard McBrien, *Catholicism,* new ed. (San Francisco: HarperSanFrancisco, 1994).
4. McBrien, *Catholicism,* p. 1077.
5. McBrien, *Catholicism,* pp. 1078-81.
6. McBrien, *Catholicism,* p. 1083.
7. McBrien, *Catholicism,* p. 1083.
8. McBrien, *Catholicism,* p. 1085.

Mediator, but believed that men and women might be afraid of him because he is also their God and Judge. Thus Mary would be an efficacious mediator.[9] Earlier we mentioned the views of people of this period of history like Anselm, Aquinas, and Scotus, who followed a scholastic method in their approach to Mary.

During the period between the Reformation and the nineteenth century an extreme position was advocated by Louis-Marie Grignion de Montfort (1673-1716), who said that true devotion to the Blessed Virgin required "absolute surrender to Mary as mystics had surrendered themselves to Christ. This, he argued, was the only effective way to Christ."[10]

As we have done, McBrien reviewed the history of Mary and Marian devotion through the nineteenth and twentieth centuries, and in doing this, he included John Henry Newman, the definitions of Mary's Immaculate Conception and her Assumption into Heaven, as well as Vatican II's role in clarifying Catholic teaching on this issue. At the end of his review he addressed the question of the theological criteria for Marian devotions. McBrien tried to avoid the extremes of maximizing and minimizing her role. He set down the following norms:

1. Devotion to Mary is ultimately devotion to Christ.
2. Jesus Christ in his humanity and divinity alike is the one Mediator between God and humanity.
3. Divine grace can work through other visible, material, bodily realities, including fellow creatures.
4. God saves us not just as individuals but as members of a people.
5. Mary is, by reason of her faith and obedience to the Word of God, a model of the Church and its preeminent member.
6. Insofar as Mary is truly the mother of Jesus Christ, she can be called the "God-bearer." She is a model for the Church in that the Church, too, is a "reality imbued with the hidden presence of God" (Pope Paul VI).
7. Just as the Church is not itself the kingdom of God, so Mary is not herself the mediator or the redeemer, even though she is the mother of Jesus and bears the incarnate Word within her.
8. Mary is, before all else, one of the redeemed.

9. McBrien, *Catholicism*, p. 1086.
10. McBrien, *Catholicism*, p. 1090.

9. While a Catholic will normally accept the Marian dogmas without res-
   ervation, it is less important *that* one affirms or denies them than *why*
   one affirms them or denies them (e.g., Thomas Aquinas denied the
   Immaculate Conception because he thought it might detract from the
   universality of the redemption).
10. Apparitions, visions, and other unusual occurrences attributed di-
    rectly to Mary may or may not be believed. None of them can ever be
    regarded as essential to Christian faith. If these phenomena do have
    any final authority, they are authoritative only for those who directly
    and immediately experience them.
11. In any case, the "contents" (messages, directives, etc.) of such events
    can never be placed on par with the gospel itself, either in terms of
    their authority or in terms of the attention they elicit and/or de-
    mand.[11]

McBrien believes that Mary does have a role in the Church today. She
is the mother all Christians insofar as she is the mother of Jesus Christ. She
was conceived without sin and in the fullness of grace, as the Church was.
"The universe of grace is a *mediated* reality: mediated principally by
Christ, and secondarily by the Church and other signs and instruments of
salvation beyond the Church. The Catholic understands the role of Mary
in salvation and accepts it because the Catholic already understands and
accepts the principle of mediation as applied in the incarnation and in the
life and mission of the Church."[12] McBrien concluded that "devotion to
Mary is consequent upon the fact that we are united with her, as with one
another, in and with Christ. She is the preeminent member of the community of saints by reason of her unique relationship with Christ, but she is a
member nonetheless, and the most exalted one at that. Our unity with her
is an expression of our unity in and with Christ."[13]

Over the centuries Catholics have expressed their devotion to Mary by
constructing shrines to her. We have already mentioned Lourdes in France
and Fátima in Portugal. Lourdes was visited by Pope Benedict XVI in 2008
to commemorate the appearances of Mary over 150 years ago. Likewise
Fátima in Portugal is a place of devotion that memorializes the 1917 ap-

11. McBrien, *Catholicism*, pp. 1106-7.
12. McBrien, *Catholicism*, p. 1108.
13. McBrien, *Catholicism*, p. 1109.

pearances of Mary to the three children. Mexico City has been the site of pilgrimages to Our Lady of Guadalupe from all over the world since the sixteenth century. The number of people who visit these places is large; for instance, over five million people each year visit Lourdes. Other notable shrines include Our Lady of Walsingham (which goes back to the eleventh century) located in Norfolk, England; the Black Madonna of Czestochowa in Poland (which goes back to at least the thirteenth century); and the shrine of Knock in County Mayo, Ireland (which dates back to the nineteenth century).

One of the most controversial shrines is that of Our Lady of Medjugorje. Medjugorje, a small town in Bosnia and Herzegovina, is a place where, since 1981, Mary has reportedly appeared to six people ("visionaries") and given each ten secrets that reveal events that will take place in the near future. The tenor of Mary's appearances was that of spreading peace and love. Since 1981 millions of people have visited this shrine. The Vatican has not taken an official position as to whether these are supernatural revelations and appearances of Mary, but has encouraged people to remember that this devotion be considered in light of the Church's official stance toward devotion to Mary.

One modern Catholic commentator on Scripture was the late Raymond Brown (1928-1998). In a chapter of one of his books titled "The Meaning of Modern New Testament Studies for an Ecumenical Understanding of Mary,"[14] he said: "Since Vatican II it has been popular in Roman Catholicism to speak of a hierarchy of truth or dogmas. To theologians this means a gradation of doctrines wherein some are recognized as more central to Christianity than others. . . . The Marian dogmas, except when primarily Christological (e.g., Mary as the Mother of God), would also be far down the list, reflecting the application of redemptive grace within the Church to its most prominent citizen. Vatican II recognized this by incorporating the treatment of Mary into its treatment of the Church."[15] Of course, in making this statement, Brown was speaking of a hierarchy of beliefs whose centrality is the Christian mystery, not devotional impact. He says of the latter: "In a hierarchy based on ecclesiastical identity, an acceptance of the Papacy would be at the very top for Roman

---

14. This is found in his book *Biblical Reflections on Crises Facing the Church* (New York: Paulist, 1975).

15. Brown, *Biblical Reflections*, p. 84.

Catholics (even as the inspiration of Scripture might be at the top for some Protestants). In a hierarchy based on devotional impact, the Marian dogmas might be near the top for Roman Catholics."[16]

Brown analyzed the passages in Scripture where Mary appears. He then summed up his conclusions: "I find confirmed more than I have ever expected Pannenberg's contention that the NT does not give us much knowledge of Mary as historical. What are we to say then, of his contention that symbolism, not history, is the key to Mariology? To some that may seem an impoverishment, but Pannenberg himself insists that there is nothing impoverished about symbolism. It has as much value as history but a different kind of value. . . . But precisely because we do not know much about the historical character and individuality of Mary, she lends herself more freely than Jesus does to a symbolic trajectory."[17] Brown gives examples of this Marian symbolism that has been used: a disciple at the annunciation and at the foot of the cross; the ideal of carrying one's cross; the model of women who were withdrawing into the Egyptian desert to lead the life of hermits; the perfect nun; the fair lady of the knights ("Our Lady"); the tender mother caring for her spiritual children; mother of the model family of Nazareth; model of the liberated woman. These are some ideals of Christian discipleship over the centuries.[18]

Brown ended his chapter by quoting Pope Paul VI's exhortation, *Marialis Cultus*:

> The Virgin Mary has always been proposed to the faithful by the church as an example to be imitated not precisely in the type of life she led, and much less for the socio-cultural background in which she lived and which today scarcely exists anywhere. Rather, she is held up as an example to the faithful for the way in which in her own particular life she fully and responsibly accepted the will of God, because she heard the word of God and acted on it, and because charity and a spirit of service were the driving force of her actions. She is worthy of imitation because she was the first and the most perfect of Christ's disciples.[19]

16. Brown, *Biblical Reflections*, p. 85.
17. Brown, *Biblical Reflections*, pp. 105-6.
18. Brown, *Biblical Reflections*, p. 107.
19. Brown, *Biblical Reflections*, p. 108.

Some concluding thoughts are in order. In our brief historical over-view of Mary's role in Catholic belief since the Reformation, we have seen the pendulum swing back and forth between 1517 and 1965. Much of the discussion centered on the "Scripture/Tradition" relationship. This was seen in both popular devotions and official Church teachings. "Tradition" seemed to be leading a life apart from Scripture, and reading Scripture did not play a big role in the life of the average Catholic. After two world wars in the first part of the twentieth century, Christians renewed their focus on what united them rather than on what divided them. As part of that reassessment done in the second half of the twentieth century, many Catholic bishops and theologians believed that they needed to rethink their position on the role of Mary in light of developments during the past four hundred years, especially as people were showing a renewed interest in biblical scholarship. Pope John XXIII (1958-1963) brought to-gether bishops and theological experts from all over the world at the Second Vatican Council (1962-1965). He also invited leading Protestant "observers" to attend.

Although many outstanding theologians were advisors at that ecumenical council, let us highlight the insights of three of them whose views influenced the decisions of the Council with regard to the role of Mary for people today. At the time of this writing, one of the leading "experts" from the Vatican II era, Joseph Ratzinger, is now Pope Benedict XVI.

In the 1940s Henri de Lubac (1896-1991) helped to found *Sources Chrétiennes* ("Christian Sources"), which provided translations (into French) of critical editions of early Christian texts and Fathers of the Church. He was one of those most responsible for the call at Vatican II to return to sources ("ressourcement") when the Council was considering how best to present current Church teaching. In his book published before Vatican II, *The Splendor of the Church*,[20] he examined the relationship between Mary and Christ, and Mary and the Church, since the very role of the Church is to bear Christ to the world today. Others after him picked up this manner of considering the role of Mary.

Not only did Karl Rahner (1904-1984) actively participate in the development of Vatican II's documents (especially the one on the Church), but he also influenced how those documents treated the role of Mary.

20. The original, French edition appeared in 1953 as *Méditation sur l'église* (Paris: Aubier).

Starting with the basic principle that Christian dogma has a history, Rahner applied this to the changing image of Mary in the Church. He was concerned to purify Mariology from pious exaggerations and speculations. In his view, mariological statements pertain to a particular individual, a historical and finite human being, who has a definite (albeit unique) place in humankind as a whole and in its history. Just as in Christology there has developed a "Christology from below," something similar could happen in Mariology. Rahner held that "Mariology from below," when developed with the more classical Mariology, could make it easier for contemporary believers to identify with Mary as a real person and a model of discipleship.[21]

Joseph Ratzinger (1927- ), the present Pope, worked closely with Karl Rahner during the four years of Vatican II. Both were advisors to the German and Austrian bishops in making suggestions for the formulation of the documents that were voted upon by the assembly. Rather recently, he said:

If, therefore, Christ and *ecclesia* are the hermeneutical center of the scriptural narration of the history of God's saving dealings with man, then and only then is the place fixed where Mary's motherhood becomes theologically significant as the ultimate personal concretization of Church. At the moment when she pronounces her Yes, Mary is Israel in person; she is the Church in person and as a person. She is the personal concretization of the Church because her *Fiat* makes her the bodily mother of the Lord. But this biological fact is a theological reality, because it realizes the deepest spiritual content of the Covenant that God intended to make with Israel.[22]

As Pope, Ratzinger best formulates the official stance of the Catholic Church on the role of Mary at the beginning of the twenty-first century.

---

21. Declan Marmion, *A Spirituality of Everyday Faith: A Theological Investigation of the Notion of Spirituality in Rahner* (Grand Rapids: Eerdmans, 1999), p. 356.
22. "Retrieving the Tradition: Thoughts on the Place of Marian Doctrine and Piety in Faith and Theology as a Whole," *Communio: International Review* 30 (2003): 155.

## Tim Perry

As I come to the end of this survey, I would offer my own concluding observations alongside those of Fr. Kendall. Five suggest themselves to me.

The first is diametrically opposed to one drawn by Fr. Kendall, above. Namely, where he sees that at least some Catholic biblical scholars have come to see the Bible attenuating widely accepted Marian belief and practice, I see a growing acknowledgment among Protestant biblical scholars and theologians that the Bible — and especially the Gospel of Luke — says much more about Mary than we have recognized since the first generation of the Reformation. Ironically, furthermore, this acknowledgment appears particularly pronounced among those Protestants for whom connectedness to the Reformation is especially strong: evangelicals. This is not to say that there is, or is about to be, a surge of Marian devotion among younger evangelicals, or that the polemical tropes first advanced by Calvin and others have completely abated. Rather, it is simply to acknowledge that many of us are returning again to the sources *(ad fontes!)* only to find that our own theological traditions have failed to speak where Scripture does. It will do us little good to criticize our Catholic brothers and sisters for speaking where Scripture is silent if we, in turn, are guilty of the opposite sin.

And so perhaps we can go at least partway with John Paul II in *Redemptoris Mater,* his gracious invitation extended to the ecclesial communities of the fractured West as much as to the churches of the East, to gather together around the sacred page to discern just what it does in fact say about Mary. For there, we may allow it to discipline both our speech and our silence. There, in the grace of our common Lord and in the power of the Holy Spirit, we may begin to sketch common ground. As will become clear below, I do not mean by this a capitulation by anyone interested in this question. Even as we gather together at the Scriptures, Fr. Kendall and I, for example, will not reach concord on their interpretation. On our own, at least. But together we serve another who prayed that we would be one. Immersion in the Scriptures on all sides, in my view, is the best way to open ourselves up to the Spirit's answer to our Lord's prayer of John 17. So I have learned to submit myself again to the witness of the Scriptures, which according to my own church tradition contain all things needful for salvation, only to find that they say much more about the Blessed Mother of God than I possibly could have imagined.

I have learned, second, that medieval theologians were decidedly not innovative in their Marian theological reflection. They inherited both edifice and scaffolding from the Fathers, and especially from Augustine. Their mariological work is to be read as an attempt to better ground mariological belief and practice through close readings of Scripture and of those Fathers to whom they had access, and to fill in the inherited scaffolding through careful, disciplined use of both deductive and inductive logic. To be sure, they are far more willing than those of us on the far side of Wittenberg to grant a place for the festivals and worship of the church as theological sources and norms. This remains, I believe, their principal error on Mary as on other theological matters. And yet, those evangelicals turning again to the Fathers for guidance will do well to remember that the "medieval" Marian positions they reject were not invented by Anselm, Aquinas, Bonaventure, Duns Scotus, or Suárez. They are rooted, rather, in the Fathers of the Church, East and West. At most, the medievals exposed and elaborated themes already present in the global Christian mind from much earlier times. It is both historically and theologically irresponsible to pit the Fathers against the medievals in broad and sharp ways.

Third, especially as a result of investigating the *theotokos* debate again, I have discovered the deep connection between Mariology and Christology. Rightly or wrongly, as both John Henry Cardinal Newman and John Calvin understood, "Mother of God" was and remains essentially a Christological title, intending to affirm the full and single personhood of the man who is God even as it also underwrites the Marian piety that made both of them cringe. Their responses were diametrically opposed. Calvin advocated a preemptive strategy, contending that the title ought to be avoided lest it promote superstition; Newman, on the other hand, was willing to allow greater freedom in devotional expression, insisting that abuses be corrected only if and as they arose. With respect to the interconnectedness of Mariology and Christology, it seems to me, the history of Christological reflection within Protestantism has vindicated Newman's course. That is to say, the stunning mariological silence in Protestantism from the days of Protestant orthodoxy to Schleiermacher seems to run hand in glove with the steady loss of Protestantism's purchase on an orthodox understanding of the person of Jesus. Of course, this is precisely what Desiderius Erasmus prophesied would happen in his satirical letter from Mary to the Reformer, Glaucoplutus, in which he described the revenge Mary would take for scrubbing churches clean of her veneration. She would, he said, go and take her child with her. It is not, therefore, surprising that the Christological and Trinitarian resurgence in Protestantism should contain a mariological resurgence as well, beginning with Karl Barth's defense of the Christological necessity not only of the *theotokos,* but also of the *natus ex virgine.* Though he refuses to follow Barth down this path, Wolfhart Pannenberg is right to say that these actions recommit Protestant theology to the path of mariological reflection. To recover a theologically and spiritually rich doctrine of the person of Christ is, inevitably, to recover Mary. Just as in the Gospel of Matthew, the Mother and her Child come together. Or they do not come.

Barth, of course, is the pivotal figure not simply because of his recovery of Mary for Protestantism, but also because he correctly discerns the core of the ongoing debate about Marian piety and the doctrines — especially the modern dogmas — that flow from it. The issue is not — pace some ongoing fundamentalist anti-Marian polemic — over the deification of Mary, but over the continuing humanity of her Son. I find it hard to argue against the point that, as especially the medieval imagination's purchase on the humanity of Jesus receded, the thoroughly human yet exalted Mary filled the void, providing believers not only with an accessible example but, to recontextualize the words of Hebrews, with a model who sympathizes with us in our weakness, yet *without sin* (cf. Heb. 4:15). Barth avers that, once our grasp on the full humanity of Christ is recovered and the words of Hebrews are given their proper object, Marian difficulties simply wither away. I have yet to find a convincing rebuttal to this charge. Thus, the fourth point, theological separation between Protestants and Catholics over Mary, is bound to persist for some time yet.

And yet, this cannot be my final word. For if Fr. Kendall and I must continue to disagree about this (among other) fundamental issues, we are agreed about the last one: Mary is a model disciple for all believers. Here, I must confess that I — along with many of my Protestant sisters and brothers — suffer from a lack of nerve rooted, ironically enough, in a peculiar atrophy of our biblical imagination. For the notion that Mary is the first Christian or the model disciple is not an invention of the medievals, and still less, the Fathers. It is the witness of the New Testament, and especially of Luke/Acts. Mary wholly receives the Word of the Lord, conforming both her will and body to it. Her "let it be" is a full and free acceptance of the will of God based entirely on simple trust in that God. As a result, not only does she speak the Word in her Magnificat; she bears it in her womb. She does so despite not having a full understanding of just what that Word means or implies for her life. Rather, she continues to ponder its meaning, both as the miraculous events surrounding the birth of her Son unfold around and in her and as she fades into obscurity and ambiguity in the later chapters of Luke's Gospel. Her named inclusion among the disciples awaiting the promise of the Father (Acts 1:14) tells us that her life of receiving, obeying, and pondering survived her uniquely dark night of the soul. And so, she is or ought to be, even for the most firmly convinced Protestant, a model after which to pattern our own lives of discipleship to her Son, our Savior and hers.

# II. ANNOTATED BIBLIOGRAPHY

# 5. Bibliography of English Language Works on Mary

Following the pattern set in previous volumes in this series, this annotated bibliography is selective according to three main criteria. First, in order to be included here a work must be significant in terms of its contribution to the development of Marian doctrine. Minor and secondary works (e.g., surveys) are excluded, though the important ones have been listed in the bibliography found at the end of the introductory essay. Second, in order to be included here a work must be relatively readily available either by purchase order, through libraries, or electronically (e.g., through www.ccel.org). Third, in order to be included here works must be in English translation.

## 1. The Fathers

With the exception of Jerome, the Fathers leave us with no lengthy treatments of Mary. Rather, their contributions are scattered across their writings and are both dogmatic and devotional in nature — sometimes, at the same time. This has made compiling a bibliography challenging. For more detailed exposition and citations of works including specific page or paragraph numbers, students are directed to the notes in the preceding essay. Here, space requires that we treat only general themes. All *ANF* and *NPNF* titles can be accessed online at http://www.ccel.org.

Ambrose of Milan. *Ambrose: Select Works and Letters*, in *NPNF*[2] 10; "The Sacrament of the Incarnation of Our Lord," in *Saint Ambrose: Seven*

*Exegetical Works,* FC 65; "The Patriarchs," in *Saint Ambrose: Seven Exegetical Works,* FC 65; "Synodal Letters," in *Saint Ambrose: Letters 1-91,* FC 26; "Letters to Priests," in *Saint Ambrose: Letters 1-91,* FC 26.

Ambrose stands with Jerome and Augustine as one of the three most impor-tant Western contributors to the Church's understanding of Mary. A staunch defender of Mary's perpetual virginity, Ambrose develops his views in contra-distinction to those of Helvidius and Jovinian. Like Tertullian before them, they held that Mary enjoyed sexual relations with Joseph after the birth of Je-sus and had other children. For Ambrose, Mary is the pristine example of consecrated virginity, and while marriage is good, the celibacy she exemplifies is a higher vocation. His reluctance to use the term "Mother of God" likely re-flects a desire to avoid possible comparison to *Magna Mater* (Great Mother) cults.

Anonymous. "The Protevangelium of James," in *The Apocryphal New Testa-ment,* edited by J. K. Elliott (Oxford: Clarendon, 1993), pp. 48-67.

This anonymous work composed in the mid-second century gives us valu-able insight into emergent Marian popular belief and piety of the second century. It fills in many of the background details of Mary's life (e.g., the names of her parents) and evinces a growing emphasis on Mary's virginity as a key element in the Annunciation and Nativity stories. In many ways, its ex-altation of Mary (and more specifically, her virginal purity) reflects a strik-ing departure from many of the Fathers, for whom Mary is the human guar-antor of a human savior.

Athanasius. "Four Discourses Against the Arians," in $NPNF^2$ 4: 306-447; "On the Incarnation of the Word," in $NPNF^2$ 4: 36-67; "Letters of Athana-sius," in $NPNF^2$ 4: 500-581.

By the time of the late third and early fourth centuries, the term *theotokos* is in circulation in Alexandria and is frequently deployed by Athanasius for his Christological purpose of defending the full deity of God the Son. In a man-ner similar to St. Antony of Egypt, Mary also serves Athanasius as an example of chastity and devotion to the then growing numbers of young monks and nuns in Egypt and elsewhere. Though he defends as a matter of biblical rec-ord both *ante partum* and *post partum* virginity, his use of the word *aiparthenos* (ever-virgin) is disputed on textual grounds; he appears to deny virginity *in partu* while defending the true deity of the Son. Of particular note is his reference to "The Commemoration of Mary," a Christian feast, as a theological criterion.

Augustine. "Of Holy Virginity," in *NPNF*[1] 3: 417-38; "Reply to Faustus the Manichean," in *NPNF*[1] 4: 151-345; "A Treatise on the Merits and Forgiveness of Sins and on the Baptism of Infants," in *NPNF*[1] 5: 11-78; "On Nature and Grace," in *NPNF*[1] 5: 115-51; "On Marriage and Concupiscence," in *NPNF*[1] 5: 258-308.

It is very difficult to draw lines with respect to Augustine. Not only is he like every other Father (Jerome excepted) in that his remarks about Mary are found throughout his writings, but other writings, such as those on baptism and original sin, exerted influence on the development of Marian thought in Western Christianity. The documents above should therefore be treated as only a very small selection that, hopefully, will lead readers into more detailed analysis of Augustine's thought (and especially his sermons). With Augustine — who surpasses both Ambrose and Jerome in influence — Western Marian thought comes into its final form. With respect to Marian developments (as with much of Western theology in general), the medieval era in the West is rightly seen as both building on an Augustinian foundation and erecting within an Augustinian superstructure.

Basil of Caesarea. "Letter CCLXI: To the Sozopolitans," in *NPNF*[2] 8: 300-301; "The Hexameron," in *NPNF*[2] 8: 52-107; "Letter CCLX: To Optimus the Bishop," in *NPNF*[2] 8: 297-99; "On the Spirit," in *NPNF*[2] 8: 2-49.

As with Gregory of Nazianzus and Gregory of Nyssa, his fellow Cappadocians, for Basil Mary functions christologically in two ways. She is, by virtue of the reality of her motherhood, a guarantee of the humanity of the Lord; her perpetual virginity at the same time is a sign pointing to his deity. She thus functions as a safeguard for an orthodox doctrine of the incarnation. She is also an exemplar for consecrated virginity and a powerful intercessor.

Chrysostom, John. *Saint Chrysostom: Homilies on the Gospel of Saint Matthew, NPNF*[1] *10; Saint Chrysostom: Homilies on the Gospel of St. John and the Epistle to the Hebrews, NPNF*[1] *14; St. John Chrysostom: Commentary on the Psalms 1,* translated by Robert Charles Hill (Brookline, MA: Holy Cross Orthodox Press, 1998).

Much of Chrysostom's Marian thought is decidedly unremarkable, not least because it mainly arises in sermons, rather than in extensive theological treatments. What some readers might find noteworthy is the ease with which he can both exalt Mary and deploy her as an example of bad behavior. While this is a fairly common dialectic in Eastern thought, the notion of Mary as, at times, mistaken or even sinful is increasingly muted in the West.

Cyril of Alexandria. "Against Nestorius," in Norman Russell, *Cyril of Alexandria* (London: Routledge, 2000), pp. 131-32; *A Commentary upon the Gospel According to S. Luke by S. Cyril, Patriarch of Alexandria*, translated by R. Payne Smith (Oxford: Oxford University Press, 1849), accessible at http://www.ccel.org/ccel/cyril/stluke.i.html; "The Third Ecumenical Council: The Council of Ephesus," in *NPNF*[2] 14: 191-242; *Cyril of Alexandria: Select Letters*, edited and translated by Lionel R. Wickham (Oxford: Oxford University Press, 1983).

Without a doubt, Cyril is Mary's great champion from among the Fathers for his defense of the term *theotokos* (Mother of God) in the Nestorian controversy that culminated in the Council of Ephesus. For him, as for Alexandrian Christology since at least Athanasius, the term functioned christologically as a guarantee of the deity, humanity, and unity of the Savior. Cyril also has a rich, almost flowery, Marian piety, to which his sermons attest. Like other Eastern theologians, however, his exaltation of Mary did not inhibit him from attributing fault to her at points.

Gregory Nazianzen. "The Third Theological Oration: On the Son," in *NPNF*[2] 7: 301-9; "To Cledonius the Priest Against Apollinarius," in *NPNF*[2] 7: 439-43; "Oration XXXVIII: On the Theophany, or Birthday of Christ," in *NPNF*[2] 7: 345-51.

As with Basil of Caesarea and Gregory of Nyssa, his fellow Cappadocians, for Nazianzen Mary functions christologically in two ways. She is, by virtue of the reality of her motherhood, a guarantee of the humanity of the Lord; her perpetual virginity at the same time is a sign pointing to his deity. She thus functions as a safeguard for an orthodox doctrine of the incarnation. She is also an exemplar for consecrated virginity and a powerful intercessor.

Gregory of Nyssa. *Commentary on the Song of Songs*, translated by Casimir McCambley, OCSO (Brookline, MA: Hellenic College Press, 1987); *The Life of Moses*, translated by Abraham J. Malherbe and Everett Ferguson, The Classics of Western Spirituality: A Library of the Great Spiritual Masters (Mahwah, NJ: Paulist, 1978); "Letter XVII: To Eustathia, Ambrosia, and Basilissa," in *NPNF*[2] 5: 197-201.

As with Basil of Caesarea and Gregory Nazianzen, his fellow Cappadocians, for Gregory of Nyssa Mary functions christologically in two ways. She is, by virtue of the reality of her motherhood, a guarantee of the humanity of the Lord; her perpetual virginity at the same time is a sign pointing to his deity. She thus functions as a safeguard for an orthodox doctrine of the incarnation. She is also an exemplar for consecrated virginity and a powerful intercessor.

Ignatius of Antioch. "Letters of Ignatius," in *The Apostolic Fathers*, vol. 1, translated and edited by Bart D. Erhman, Loeb Classical Library, vol. 24 (Cambridge, MA: Harvard University Press, 2005 [2003]), pp. 201-322.

Composed around 110 CE, the letters of Ignatius contain the earliest extant references to the Blessed Virgin Mary outside the Bible. Writing as a pastor worried about the advance of false teaching denying the humanity of Jesus — whom Ignatius calls "our God" — Ignatius deploys Mary and the reality of her motherhood to affirm the *real* and therefore *saving* humanity and suffering of her Son.

Irenaeus. "Against Heresies," in *ANF* 1: 315-567; *On the Apostolic Preaching*, translated by John Behr (Crestwood, NY: St. Vladimir's Seminary Press, 1997).

Irenaeus is the first Christian writer to develop the Mary/Eve typology in any detail, emphasizing the activity of Mary in the plan of salvation, and going so far as to call her Eve's "advocate." Although his exalted language clearly exceeds both that of the New Testament and earlier writers, he does not think of Mary as immune to fault. Nevertheless, he denies that he is an innovator in any way, but merely stands in the tradition of the Apostles, having been trained by their first students.

Jerome. "The Perpetual Virginity of Blessed Mary: Against Helvidius," in *NPNF*[2] 6: 335-46; *Homilies Volume 2 (Homilies 60-96)*, FC 57.

Jerome stands with Ambrose and Augustine as one of the three most important Western contributors to the Church's understanding of Mary. A staunch defender of Mary's perpetual virginity, Jerome develops his views in contradistinction to those of Helvidius and Jovinian. Like Tertullian before them, they held that Mary enjoyed sexual relations with Joseph after the birth of Jesus and had other children. For Jerome, Mary is the pristine example of consecrated virginity, and while marriage is good, the celibacy she exemplifies is a higher vocation. What sets Jerome apart from Ambrose and Augustine is his insistence on grounding long-accepted traditional Marian beliefs in his close exegesis of Holy Scripture. "The Perpetual Virginity of Blessed Mary: Against Helvidius" is the most important of Jerome's works, though the entirety of *NPNF*[2] vol. 6, *Jerome: Letters and Select Works*, is important.

Justin Martyr. "Dialogue with Trypho," in *ANF* 1: 194-270.

Writing in the second century, Justin is the first Christian author for which we have evidence who compares Mary to Eve. This motif will be taken up and explored to great effect by Irenaeus and Tertullian. For Roman Catholics, the logical and theological conclusion of this avenue of exploration is the dogma of the Immaculate Conception.

Origen. "Against Celsus," in *ANF* 4: 395-428; "Origen's Commentary on the Gospel of Matthew," in *ANF* 9: 409-512; *Homilies on Leviticus*, FC 83.

Origen makes use of the Mary/Eve typology and explicitly defends Mary's virginity *post partum*. He highlights her perpetual virginity because it is fitting that consecrated virgins should have their own example. He follows in a tradition whose first recorded exponent was Ignatius of Antioch in explaining Mary's marriage to Joseph as part of an elaborate divine deception to conceal the identity of Jesus from the Devil.

Tertullian. "Five Books Against Marcion," in *ANF* 3: 271-475; "On the Flesh of Christ," in *ANF* 3: 521-43; "On Monogamy," in *ANF* 4: 59-73; "On the Veiling of Virgins," in *ANF* 4: 27-38.

In addition to deploying the Mary/Eve typology in ways slightly different to those of Irenaeus, Tertullian strongly emphasizes the reality of Mary's motherhood as a means of stressing the humanity of the Lord. He insists that Mary and Joseph's marriage included full sexual relations, resulting in the births of those whom the NT calls Jesus' brothers and sisters. He holds Mary up as an example to both consecrated virgins and wives. With her example, Mary hallows both celibacy and marriage.

## 2. The Medieval Era and the Reformation

Anselm of Canterbury. "Of the Virgin Conception and Original Sin," in *Theological Treatises*, edited by Jasper Hopkins and Herbert Richardson (Cambridge: Harvard Divinity Library, 1967); "Cur Deus Homo," in *Basic Writings*, edited by Charles Hartshorne (La Salle, IL: Open Court, 1962).

Anselm is among the first to reflect at length on the relationship between the sinlessness of Mary and Jesus, speculating early on that there is a necessary connection, but finally concluding that it is one of fittingness. As the special vessel chosen by the Father to bear the Son through the overshadowing of the Holy Spirit, the notion of Mary sinning is simply inconceivable. Though, hewing closely to Augustine, he does not believe in the Immaculate Conception, he takes a definitive step toward the doctrine in his argument that

Mary's holiness was accomplished in anticipation of the saving work of her Son.

Luther, Martin. "Commentary on the Magnificat," in *The Sermon on the Mount and Magnificat*, LW 21: 297-358.

Throughout his long life and many works, Martin Luther displayed a warm-hearted Marian piety that emerges throughout his literary corpus. At the same time, from 1517 on, he displays a growing vehemence with respect to certain Marian pious practices that, he believes, shift the believer's focus away from the loving Savior, or worse, transmogrify him into the "Angry Judge." In addition, with respect to Marian doctrines — the *theotokos*, Mary's virginity and holiness and so on — Luther remains from first to last thoroughly catholic. His one moment of originality occurs in his commentary on the Magnificat, where Mary is presented as the model of justification by faith alone.

Suárez, Francis. *The Dignity and Virginity of the Mother of God* (West Baden Springs, IN: West Baden College, 1954).

This book translates the first, fifth, and sixth disputations of the *Mysteries of the Life of Christ* since "they treat what Suárez and most Catholic theologians consider Mary's fundamental privileges, that of Mother and Virgin" (p. ix). Well versed in the Scriptures, the Fathers, and the medieval theologians, Suárez is a pristine example of the scholastic approach to Mary (and indeed to theology in general) that would dominate Catholic thought from the Council of Trent until the Second Vatican Council.

Thomas Aquinas. *Compendium of Theology*, translated by Cyril Vollert (St. Louis: B. Herder, 1948); *Summa Theologiae*, vol. 51: *Our Lady*, translated by Thomas R. Heath (New York: McGraw-Hill, 1969).

Although Thomas was quite rightly regarded as a revolutionary theologian for shifting Western theology's metaphysic from Neo-Platonism to Aristotle, his Marian reflections are remarkable for their unoriginality. His work, rather than breaking new ground, is focused on clearing up misunderstandings and ironing out wrinkles he has found in previous generations of Marian devotees. Thomas is especially remembered for his endorsement of Bernard of Clairvaux's opposition to the doctrine of the Immaculate Conception. In Thomas's view, the saving work of Christ would not be universal in scope were Mary to be conceived without original sin. The *Compendium of Theology* expresses Thomas's Marian thought in compressed form. A fuller treatment is found in vol. 51 of the *Summa Theologiae*.

## 3. Modern Contributions

Balasuriya, Tissa, OMI. *Mary and Human Liberation: The Story and the Text*, edited by Helen Stanton (Harrisburg, PA: Trinity Press International, 1997).

Like early feminist theologians, this postcolonial Asian theologian sought to develop Mariology in ways suited to the experience of men and women in South Asia. His combative style and apparent denial of Mary's virginity culminated in his (long-rescinded) excommunication from the Catholic Church in 1997.

Balthasar, Hans Urs von. *Mary for Today* (San Francisco: Ignatius, 1988).

One of the most influential theologians for John Paul II and Benedict XVI, Hans Urs von Balthasar draws on the Scriptures and ancient theological resources to offer a rich and traditional presentation of Mary as the Church in crucible and as a model for believers.

Barth, Karl. "The Miracle of Christmas," in *CD* I/2: 172-202.

While Mary is treated at other places in Barth's many writings, this offers the most extensive and complete account, of which the others are merely reiterations. Barth marks a distinctive break with the silence of liberal Protestantism in three ways. Over against his fellow Protestants, he insists upon the Christological necessity of *theotokos* as a Marian title and is equally determined to reintroduce the Virgin Birth as a proper subject of theological contemplation, signifying as it does the utter helplessness of all human beings before the grace of God. Similarly, against Catholicism, he is equally vociferous about any Marian doctrine or pious practice that decouples Mary from Christ and elevates her to a second center of salvation.

Beattie, Tina. *God's Mother, Eve's Advocate: A Marian Narrative of Women's Salvation* (New York: Continuum, 2002).

A convert to Catholicism from Presbyterian Christianity, Beattie represents a new move among younger feminist theologians who seek to empower women not by moving away from the traditional portrayal of Mary, but by embracing and expanding it. Such an expansion is conducted here through a creative engagement with French postmodern and psychoanalytic theory.

Boff, Leonardo. *Mary: The Maternal Face of God* (Maryknoll, NY: Orbis, 1987).

Boff's attempt to reflect on Mary in a way that would do justice to the experience of the Latin American Church results in a Mary who in many ways resembles other liberationist Marian portraits: Mary the strong, faithful disciple. Rather than criticizing the tradition, however, Boff stretches it. Because he presents Mary as Christ's equal and even as a hypostatization of the Holy Spirit, conservatives and liberals alike have criticized his approach for the way in which it de-centers the saving person and work of Jesus Christ.

Jenson, Robert W. *Systematic Theology,* 2 vols. (New York: Oxford University Press, 1997, 1999); "A Space for God," in *Mary, Mother of God,* edited by Carl E. Braaten and Robert W. Jenson (Grand Rapids: Eerdmans, 2004), pp. 49-57.

Taking Barth's call to renewed Marian reflection from within ecumenically sensitive Protestantism to its maximal point, Robert Jenson defends not simply the *theotokos,* but also traditional Marian beliefs, including the modern dogmas of Immaculate Conception and Bodily Assumption.

John Paul II. "Redemptoris Mater," in *The Encyclicals of John Paul II,* translated and edited by J. Michael Miller (Huntington, IN: Our Sunday Visitor, 2001).

John Paul II's Marian piety easily equaled that of Pius IX and Pius XII. He was, at the same time, the most ecumenically sensitive Pope of the modern era. Both piety and ecumenical concern come together in this important document. It is an invitation to the Churches of the East and to the Protestant communities of the West to sit with John Paul and the Catholic Church and consider the teaching of Holy Scripture about Mary, in order to see if Mary can in fact become a basis for unity rather than an ongoing obstacle.

Johnson, Elizabeth. *Truly Our Sister: A Theology of Mary in the Communion of Saints* (New York: Continuum, 2004).

Standing in the tradition of critical feminism first enunciated by Rosemary Radford Ruether, Elizabeth Johnson nevertheless believes that feminist theology can move past criticism of Marian traditions to constructive Marian reflection. In this book, she focuses on close readings of the biblical texts, and especially the Gospels of Luke and John, to present a portrait of Mary that is, when compared to the tradition, minimal and yet attractive and relevant for modern believers. Her Mary is a model disciple, defined by her strength and persistence.

Newman, John Henry. *Certain Difficulties Felt by Anglicans in Catholic Teaching,* vol. 2 (1892; London/New York: Longman, Green, 2001); *Discourses to Mixed Congregations* (Springfield, IL: Templegate, 1964); *Meditations and Devotions of the Late Cardinal Newman,* with William Plain Neville (Whitefish, MT: Kessinger, 2007).

The most famous convert from Anglicanism, John Henry Newman is an important expositor of Marian doctrine, and especially his defense of the Immaculate Conception as the logical conclusion of the ancient ascription of the title, "the New Eve," to Mary. He is also a proponent of a more "minimal" Marian devotion, even as he acknowledges that such devotional practices are diverse and expand and contract over time and geography.

Paul VI. *Lumen Gentium,* available at http://www.vatican.va/archive/ hist_councils/ii_vatican_council/documents/vat-ii_const_19641121 _lumen-gentium_en.html; *Marialis Cultis,* available at http://www .vatican.va/holy_father/paul_vi/apost_exhortations/documents/hf _p-vi_exh_19740202_marialis-cultus_en.html.

In chapter 8 of *Lumen Gentium,* the Second Vatican Council's declaration on the Church, the bishops turn their attention to Mary. By locating her within the document on the Church (rather than giving her her own document) and by stressing the priority of the Holy Scriptures and Fathers of the undivided Church, the bishops of the Council, without denying Church teaching (including the modern dogmas), hope to present Mary to Protestant communities and to the churches of the East in a way that is not unnecessarily offensive. This is a remarkable achievement, reached with much effort and some controversy. Paul VI followed this document with an apostolic exhortation, *Marialis Cultus,* that offered practical guides to the implementation of the Council's reforms at the parish level.

Pius IX. *The Bull "Ineffabilis Deus" in Four Languages,* translated and edited by Ulick J. Bourke (Dublin: Mullany, 1868).

This is the document that declares the Immaculate Conception to be a dogma to be received by all the faithful. Its careful language rules out the notion, held by Thomists until well into the nineteenth century, that Mary was conceived in original sin and cleansed at a later time. At the same time, however, it carefully excludes extreme views holding that Mary did not need to be saved. Mary was preserved from original sin from the moment of her conception in view of the merits of Christ. This enshrines John Duns Scotus's response to Thomas Aquinas, namely, that the Immaculate Conception does not demean Christ as Savior, but in fact exalts him. For it avers that he saves not only by redemption, but also by preservation.

Pius XII. *Munificentissimus Deus,* available at http://www.vatican.va/ holy_father/pius_xii/apost_constitutions/documents/hf_p-xii_apc _19501101_munificentissimus-deus_en.html.

Capping the Marian century that opened in 1854 with the definition of the Immaculate Conception, this document defines the Bodily Assumption of the Blessed Virgin Mary into heaven as a dogma to be received by the faithful. Strikingly, the document refuses to take a position on Mary's death, saying only that she was taken into heavenly glory at the completion of her earthly life, and remains silent on Mary's status as co-redeemer with Christ.

Rahner, Karl. *Mary the Mother of Our Lord* (New York: Herder & Herder, 1963).

A major influence on the discussions that became *Lumen Gentium,* chapter 8, Karl Rahner explores the relationship between Mary and the Church in this small, important book. He presents Mary as a symbol of the Church in order to show that devotion to Mary can in no way conflict with or rival devotion to the Church, the sacraments, or the Lord.

Ruether, Rosemary Radford. "Mistress of Heaven: The Meaning of Mariology," in *New Woman, New Earth: Sexist Ideologies and Human Liberation* (New York: Seabury, 1975), pp. 36-62; *Sexism and God-Talk* (Boston: Beacon, 1983).

An early and vocal post–Vatican II critic of traditional Marian belief and practice, Ruether once suggested that, even as a symbol of corporate faith, Mary was simply irredeemable for women. As the Virgin Mother, Mary embodied an impossible ideal. Later, however, she offered a reading of the Magnificat that held open the possibility of these words grounding a liberative praxis for feminist theology. Ruether does not engage in positive mariological reflection.

Schleiermacher, Friedrich. *The Christian Faith,* 2nd ed., translated by H. R. Mackintosh and J. S. Stewart (Edinburgh: T. & T. Clark, 1928).

Schleiermacher represents the definitive break between liberal Protestantism and Catholicism over Mary. With him, the old Reformation debates about the perpetual virginity of Mary and anti-Catholic polemic are decidedly set aside. The virginal conception of the Lord, like other biblical miracles, neither contributes to nor detracts from authentic Christian commitment, the feeling of absolute dependence upon God.

# Index of Names and Subjects

# Index of Names and Subjects

Farrugia, Mario, 89
Fàtima, Portugal, appearance of Mary in, 58, 92
Feminism, 4, 76-77
*Formula of Concord,* 78

Germanus of Constantinople, 59
Grace, 46
Great Schism, 86
Gregory Nazianzus, 27-28, 31-32
Gregory of Nyssa, 27-29
Groupe des Dombes, 84
Guadalupe, Our Lady of, 50, 93

Hail Mary, 49
*Heidelberg Catechism,* 79
Helvidius, 34-35, 37-38

Ignatius of Antioch, 19-20
Immaculate Conception, 5, 41, 44-45, 53-54, 55, 58, 62, 68, 71, 73, 75, 77, 83, 85-87, 90, 91
Immaculate Heart of Mary, 58, 67
Intercession, 56, 65
Irenaeus of Lyons, 22-23, 68

Jenson, Robert W., 5, 83-84
Jerome, 32, 36-38, 41
John XXIII, 62-65, 95
John Damascene, 59
John Paul II, 73-75, 97
Johnson, Elizabeth, 76-77
Joseph, 7-8, 35, 37-38, 46
Jovinian, 34-35
Justin Martyr, 22, 55

Kniazeff, Alexis, 87
Knock, shrine of, 93

Lebedev, Alexander, 86-87
Leo the Great, 33
Liberation theology, 75-78
Lourdes, shrine of, 53, 92

Luther, Martin, 47, 48
Lutheran-Catholic Dialogue (U.S.), 84

Magnificat, 8, 49
Manicheanism, 34, 39
Marian devotion, 47, 49, 56, 64, 67, 74, 81-90
Marriage, 72-73
Mary: and the Church, 40-41, 62-65, 66, 67-71, 73, 74, 75, 90-91; and Israel, 72; and monasticism, 33, 38, 41; as mother, 24, 30, 69, 72; as prophet, 83-84; as Queen of heaven, 10, 11, 57, 62; sinlessness of, 44-45, 47, 56, 57, 86-87
McBrien, Richard, 90-91
Mediatrix, 63, 69, 71, 90
Medugorje, Our Lady of, 93
Melanchthon, Philip, 79
Meyendorf, John, 87
Montfort, Louis-Marie Grignion de, 91
More, Thomas, 47
Mother of God. *See Theotokos*

Nestorius/Nestorianism, 29, 90
New Eve, 19-43, 55, 57, 60, 61, 66, 67, 68, 71
Newman, John Henry, 51, 55-58, 98
Nicea, Council of (325), 27

O'Collins, Gerald, 89
Origen, 24
Original sin/guilt, 32, 39, 44-45, 47, 87
Orthodoxy, modern, 85-88

Pannenberg, Wolfhart, 83, 94, 99
Paul VI, 66-67, 73, 94
Pelagius/Pelagianism, 36, 39
Perpetual Virginity, 11-13, 24-25, 28, 31, 34-35, 36, 37, 38, 40-41, 46, 47, 51, 68, 72, 74, 90
Pius IX, 44-45, 53-54, 59
Pius XII, 58-61

# Index of Scripture References

9 780802 827333